Civil Government of Virginia

William F. Fox

Contents

INTRODUCTION. 7
I. GENERAL PRINCIPLES 11
II. LEGISLATIVE DEPARTMENT. 18
III. EXECUTIVE DEPARTMENT. 26
IV. EXECUTIVE DEPARTMENT--Continued. 32
V. JUDICIARY DEPARTMENT. 45
VI. JUDICIARY DEPARTMENT-Continued. 53
VII. OFFICERS OF COURTS. 60
VIII. COUNTY ORGANIZATION. 67
IX. DISTRICT ORGANIZATION. 79
X. GOVERNMENT OF CITIES AND TOWNS. 83
XI. EDUCATION. 87
OUTLINE OF COLONIAL AND STATE HISTORY. 94
COLONIAL GOVERNORS. 97
STATE GOVERNORS. 99
CONSTITUTION OF VIRGINIA. 101
ARTICLE I. BILL OF RIGHTS. 102
ARTICLE II ELECTIVE FRANCHISE AND QUALIFICATIONS FOR OFFICE 106
ARTICLE III DIVISION OF POWERS. 113
ARTICLE IV. LEGISLATIVE DEPARTMENT. 114
ARTICLE V. EXECUTIVE DEPARTMENT. 123
ARTICLE VI. JUDICIARY DEPARTMENT 128
ARTICLE VII. ORGANIZATION AND GOVERNMENT OF COUNTIES 136
ARTICLE VIII. ORGANIZATION AND GOVERNMENT OF CITIES ....
    AND TOWNS. 138
ARTICLE IX. EDUCATION AND PUBLIC INSTRUCTION. 145
ARTICLE X. AGRICULTURE AND IMMIGRATION. 149
ARTICLE XI PUBLIC INSTITUTIONS AND PRISONS. 150
ARTICLE XII. CORPORATIONS. 152
ARTICLE XIII. TAXATION AND FINANCE. 168
ARTICLE XIV. MISCELLANEOUS PROVISIONS. 177
ARTICLE XV. FUTURE CHANGES IN THE CONSTITUTION 179

CIVIL GOVERNMENT OF VIRGINIA

BY

William F. Fox

INTRODUCTION.

The word GOVERNMENT means guidance or direction or management. It means also the person or persons who rule or control any establishment or institution. Wherever any number of people live together in one house, or one town, or city, or country, there must be government of some kind.

In the family the parents are the government. They guide and manage the affairs of the house. They give orders to their children as to what they must do and what they must not do, and they see that their orders are obeyed. This is government, and it is for the benefit of the family. If the children were to do as they please, there would be no peace or happiness in the home.

And in their games and amusements out of doors children find that they must not do as they please. Every game has certain rules or laws which those who take part in it are required to obey. In the game of baseball, for example, the players are not allowed to act as they like. There are rules of the play, and there is an umpire to see that the rules are observed.

In the school, too, and in all business establishments there must be government. The teachers direct the work in their classes, giving orders to the pupils as to what lessons they must study and how they must study them. In the store and factory there is a manager or master who directs the business. If there were no managers or masters there would be nothing but disorder and confusion.

We can see therefore how necessary government is, and we can understand why it is that there must be government in the country or state in which we live. There must be laws to direct men how they must behave towards one another and to punish those who do wrong. And there must be people to make the laws and people to see that they are carried out.

This is CIVIL GOVERNMENT. The word CIVIL means pertaining to the state, or to the relations between citizens and the state, and the word STATE means the whole community or body of people living under one government.

There are different kinds of government in different countries. In some countries the government is monarchical--that is, under one person, a king or emperor--and in some countries it is republican.

A republican government, or a republic, is a government in which the chief power is exercised not by one person but by all the people. The government of the United States is a republican government. The government of Virginia is a republican government. The head of the state under a republican form of government is elected by the people.

The government in a republic is usually divided into three parts or DEPARTMENTS. One department makes the laws. This is called the LEGISLATIVE DEPARTMENT or the legislature. It is formed of a certain number of persons who are elected at certain times, by the people, and who meet to make laws that are necessary for the good of the state or country.

The second department of government is called the EXECUTIVE DEPARTMENT, and is also formed of persons who are elected by the people, and their business is to execute or carry out the laws. Their duty is to see that every one who violates any law of the country or state is brought to punishment, and that the laws made for promoting the well-being and happiness of the people are carried out.

The third department of the government is the JUDICIAL DEPARTMENT or the judiciary. Its members are, in Virginia, chosen by the legislature. Their duty is to administer the laws, that is to inquire into every case in which a person is accused of breaking the laws, and if a person is found to be guilty, to sentence him to the punishment which the law prescribes for the crime or offence he has committed.

In this book full particulars and explanations are given as to the formation of those three departments of government, the many duties assigned to each, and how those duties are performed.

In republics government is usually carried on according to the wishes of the majority of the people. This is what is called MAJORITY RULE. At elections to form the legislative or executive department, different persons or candidates are proposed for each office, and the candidate who gets a majority of the votes is elected. A candidate is a person who is proposed for election to some office.

Candidates for public offices are proposed or nominated at what are called CONVENTIONS. A convention is a meeting of electors, or voters, held for the purpose of agreeing upon or choosing persons to be candidates for office. Conventions are called together and conducted by organizations known as PARTIES or POLITICAL PARTIES. There are usually at least two political parties in every country in which there is constitutional government. Each of the parties nominates candidates at every election, and tries in every legitimate way to persuade the people to vote for its candidates.

The party whose candidates are elected is called THE PARTY IN POWER. This is what is known as PARTY GOVERNMENT.

It is good for the state that there should be political parties. Each party closely watches the conduct of the other, and if the party in power make bad laws or execute the laws unfairly or unjustly, the party out of power appeals to the people by public speeches and by writing in newspapers, and does what it can to get the voters to vote against the party in power at the next election and turn it out of office.

Every citizen may join either of the parties he pleases, and so exercise his influence through conventions and elections to secure good government. And it is the duty of every citizen to do this, for good government--honest law-makers and honest administrators of the laws--is one of the greatest blessings a state can have. It is also the duty of young people to learn about the government and politics of their state, so that when they come of age they may be able to perform their part as citizens intelligently and well.

QUESTIONS.
1. Define GOVERNMENT.
2. Give some illustrations of the necessity of government.
3. What is the necessity for laws in a country?
4. Define CIVIL.
5. What is a republic?
6. What does the government in a republic consist of?
7. What is the duty of the legislative department?
8. What is the duty of the executive department?
9. What is the duty of the judicial department?

10. What do you understand by majority rule?
11. What is a convention?
12. What is a party government?
13. Why is it good for the state that there should be political parties?
14. Why is it the duty of every citizen to become a member of one of the political parties?
15. Why is it good for young people to learn about government and politics?

I.
GENERAL PRINCIPLES

1. All power is vested in and hence derived from the people; magistrates are their trustees and servants and at all times amenable to them.

2. Government is, or ought to be, instituted for the common benefit, protection, and security of the people.

3. No free government, or the blessing of liberty, can be preserved to any people but by a firm adherence to justice, moderation, temperance, frugality, and virtue, and by frequent recurrence to fundamental principles.
--Bill of Rights.

The BILL OF RIGHTS is the title of the first article, or chapter, of the Constitution of Virginia. It is so called because it is a declaration or statement of the RIGHTS of the people in regard to government. In English history the name BILL OF RIGHTS is given to a declaration of rights adopted by the two houses of Parliament in England in 1688, and soon afterwards passed into law.

VESTED IN means entrusted to or put in possession of. To vest is to invest or clothe with power or authority.

MAGISTRATES are public officers whose duty it is to administer the laws. The President is the chief magistrate of the nation. It is his duty to see that the laws of the United States are executed Or carried out. The governor is the chief magistrate of the State; the mayor is the chief magistrate of the city. Judges are magistrates who preside in the courts and administer the law as applying to the cases brought before them.

Trustees are persons who hold or have charge of the property of others in trust, and as guardians, for those to whom it belongs. Magistrates hold their offices as trustees for the people, and they are amenable, that is, answerable, to the people. If they do not perform the duties of their offices honestly, the people can call them to account and punish them.

A FREE GOVERNMENT is a government instituted, that is, established, by the consent of the people. The government of the United States is a free government, because it has been established by the people, and the people can change it when they please.

"Government ought to be established for the COMMON BENEFIT." This means that government ought to be for the benefit of all the people, poor as well as rich, and under a free government all the people have equal protection from the law.

FUNDAMENTAL PRINCIPLES are principles or truths according to which, or upon which, systems, or laws, or institutions, are FOUNDED. The fundamental principles of free government are that all men are born equal, and that all men have equal rights to life and liberty.

RECURRENCE means A GOING BACK TO. We must frequently recur, or go back to, fundamental principles in order to preserve free government. We must also firmly adhere to, or practice justice, moderation, temperance, and virtue.

JUSTICE is the doing of what is right. MODERATION means the avoiding of severity or harshness in our conduct towards others. TEMPERANCE is the moderate or reasonable use or enjoyment of the pleasures of life. FRUGALITY is the practice of thrift and economy as opposed to extravagance. VIRTUE is the practice of the moral good taught by religion.

The constitution guarantees to the people the right to make and to change their own laws; the right of speedy trial by jury; protection in the enjoyment of their inherent rights; freedom of elections; freedom of speech; freedom of the press; religious freedom; equal civil and political rights and public privileges.

It prohibits excessive bail, excessive fines, the infliction of cruel and unusual punishments, and the taking of private property for public uses except by law and with just compensation.

A CONSTITUTION is a system or plan of government, or a written or printed statement of the principles and rules according to which a government is to be conducted. The constitution tells how the government is to be formed, what it has power to do, and what it must not do. The Constitution of Virginia GUARANTEES, that is, secures or makes sure to the people, the right to make or change the laws. A government under a constitution is called a CONSTITUTIONAL government.

TRIAL BY JURY is trial by a judge and certain citizens who are called the jury. The duty of the judge is to see that the trial is conducted according to law, and to pass sentence on the accused person if found guilty. The duty of the jury is to decide, after hearing the evidence, whether the accused person is guilty or not. This declaration of the jury is called a VERDICT, a word which means a TRUE SAYING.

INHERENT means inseparable from, or not to be taken away. INHERENT RIGHTS are rights that cannot justly be taken away from the people. The right to life and liberty is an inherent right of man which cannot be taken away by any constitution or government.

FREEDOM OF ELECTIONS means freedom to hold elections to choose the officers of government, and freedom for every citizen to vote for the candidate of his choice. FREEDOM OF SPEECH and FREEDOM OF THE PRESS mean liberty for all to speak or publish what they desire to say on any subject, being liable to punishment by law if they speak or publish anything injurious to the reputation of others. RELIGIOUS FREEDOM means liberty to belong to any religion, or to worship God in any way that one thinks proper.

CIVIL RIGHTS are the rights a man is entitled to as a member of the community, such as the right to trial by jury, the right of freedom of speech.

POLITICAL RIGHTS are the rights that belong to men as citizens, Such, as the right to vote, the right to be candidates for public office.

PUBLIC PRIVILEGES are benefits or advantages possessed by some and not by others, such as charters to corporations or licenses to carry on certain kinds of business. For example, a license to sell liquors is a public privilege. It is not for the public good that it should be given to everybody, but the Constitution guarantees that under necessary restrictions as to the number of such licenses granted, all citizens shall have equal rights to such privileges.

PRIVATE PROPERTY is property that belongs to private individuals. It may be taken for public use when necessary. If a government building has to be erected or a railroad made, the land required for the purpose may be taken from the owner, but a just price must be paid for it.

Who May Vote and Hold Office. Every male citizen of the United States, who is 21 years old, who has been a resident of the State two years, of the county, city, or town one year, and of the precinct in which he offers to vote thirty days next preceding any election, has been registered and has paid his state poll taxes, shall be entitled to vote; except idiots and lunatics, persons convicted after the adoption of the constitution of bribery in any election, embezzlement of public funds, treason, felony, or petit larceny, obtaining money or other property under false pretences, or who have been in any way concerned in a duel.

All persons entitled to vote shall be eligible to any office within the gift of the people, except as restricted by the constitution.

Excepting the requirements of residence in the voting precinct, payment of poll tax and registration, the qualifications of jurors are practically the same as those of voters.

A CITIZEN is a native of the United States or a foreigner who has been made a citizen. To be made a citizen, a person must, at least two years before admission, make a declaration before a judge that it is his intention to become a citizen of the United States, and to renounce allegiance to all foreign powers or princes. Having so declared his intention, and after residing five years in the United States, he must declare on oath before a judge that he renounces allegiance to all foreign powers, and that he will support the Constitution of the United States. He then receives a paper or document certifying that he is a citizen. The paper is called a NATURALIZATION paper, and the person who receives it is said to be NATURALIZED, because it entitles him to all the rights and privileges of a NATIVE or NATURAL-BORN citizen of the United States.

CONVICTED means tried in a public court for a crime and found guilty. BRIBERY in elections is buying or selling votes, or giving money or payment in any form to a voter for voting for any candidate. EMBEZZLEMENT is the crime a person commits who takes for his own use the money or property of others that has been entrusted to his care. TREASON is to make war against or try to overthrow or destroy the government of one's own country. FELONY is a crime that may be punished by death or imprisonment in state prison. PETIT LARCENY is the stealing of goods of small value.

Every voter is required to be registered. This is a most important proceeding, as it insures the purity of the ballot and the intelligent exercise of the right of franchise. Elections. Shall be by ballot; for State, county, corporation and district officers, shall be held the Tuesday after the first Monday in November; except for mayors and councils of cities and towns, which shall be the second Tuesday of June.

State executive officers elected at a general election shall enter upon the duties of their respective offices the first of February next thereafter; members of the House of Delegates and all county, corporation, and district officers on the first of January, and Senators on the second Wednesday in January next thereafter; and mayors and councils of cities and towns on the first of September next succeeding their election. State executive officers elected by the General Assembly enter upon their duties the first of March following their election.

They shall continue to discharge the duties of their respective offices until their successors shall have qualified.

The BALLOT is the printed list containing the names of all the candidates to be voted for at an election. The places where the people vote are called POLLS, and they are kept open for one day-- from sunrise to sunset. At the polls there are officers called judges or clerks of election. When the voter goes to the poll on election day, one of the judges hands him a ballot. With the ballot he goes alone into a small compartment or BOOTH, where there is a desk with a pencil or pen and ink. There he draws a mark with the pen or pencil through the names of the candidates he does not wish to vote for, leaving the names of the candidates he votes for unmarked He then, folds up the ballot, with the names of the candidates on the inside, and hands it to one of the judges, who drops it into a box, where it remains until the votes are counted after the poll closes. The candidates who receive the highest number of votes are declared elected. This is done by the Board of State Canvassers (which see).

STATE OFFICERS are officers elected by the voters of the whole State. The governor, the lieutenant-governor, and attorney-general are State officers.

A CORPORATION is a body or number of persons formed and authorized by law to carry on business under one name as a single person. Banks and railroad and manufacturing companies are corporations. They are called private corporations because the business they do is for the benefit of private individuals. The people of cities and towns have power by law to carry on the government of their cities and towns as corporations. They are called public corporations because they are formed for the purpose of government, and act for the whole people (see under Government of Cities and Towns)

QUALIFIED, with regard to State officers, means having taken the oath of office. The Constitution requires that every person, before entering upon the discharge of any functions as an officer of the State, must solemnly swear or affirm that he will support and maintain the Constitution and laws of the State of Virginia, and that he will faithfully perform the duty of the office to which he has been elected. To take this oath is to QUALIFY for the office.

The State is entitled to two U. S. Senators and ten Representatives in Congress, and to twelve votes for President and Vice-President in the Electoral College.

The ELECTORAL COLLEGE is the name given to the body of persons who elect the President and Vice-President of the United States. At a presidential election, which takes place every four years, the people do not vote directly for the candidates who have been nominated for President and Vice-President. They vote for persons nominated to be ELECTORS, and each State has the right to choose as many electors as it has senators and representatives in Congress. Virginia has two senators and ten representatives in Congress, therefore at the presidential election it chooses twelve electors. This is what is meant by saying that it has twelve votes in the Electoral College.

The members of the Electoral College do not meet all together to elect the President and Vice-President. The electors of each State meet in the capital of their own State in January after they are elected, and vote by ballot for President and Vice-President. after which they send lists to the President of the United States Senate showing how they have voted. Those lists are examined in the Senate and the votes counted. Then the candidates who have received the votes of a majority of the Electoral College are declared elected.

QUESTIONS.
1. From whom are the powers of government derived?
2. What are magistrates?
3. For what is government instituted?
4. What are fundamental principles?
5. What is the Bill of Rights?
6 What is a constitution?

7. What is trial by jury?

8 Tell what you understand by freedom of elections, freedom of speech, freedom of the press, and religious freedom

9. Tell the difference between civil rights and political rights.

10. What are public privileges?

11. What is involuntary servitude?

12. Define PRIVATE PROPERTY.

13. Who is entitled to vote, and who is eligible to office?

14. What is a citizen?

15. How may one become a citizen?

16. Define the terms BRIBERY, EMBEZZLEMENT, TREASON, FELONY, PETIT LARCENY, and DUEL.

17. What are jurors?

18. When are the elections for State officers held?

19. How are elections conducted?

20. Define BALLOT, POLLS, and BOOTH.

21. What are State officers?

22. What is a corporation?

23. What is the meaning of QUALIFIED?

24. How many senators and representatives in Congress is the State entitled to?

25. How many votes is the State entitled to in the Electoral College?

26. What is the Electoral College?

27. How do the electors choose the President and Vice-President of the United States?

II.
LEGISLATIVE DEPARTMENT.

The legislative power of the commonwealth is vested in a General Assembly consisting of a Senate and House of Delegates.

LEGISLATIVE POWER is the power to legislate or make LAWS, hence the General Assembly is the LEGISLATURE of Virginia. COMMONWEALTH, which means COMMON WELL-BEING, or common good, is a name sometimes given to a State or country which has a republican form of government--that is, a government in which the people are the supreme power, and in which all the people have common (that is, equal) interests and common rights. CONSISTING means formed or made up of.

A DELEGATE is a person appointed or elected by others to do business for them as their representative. The members of the House of Delegates are elected by the people of the State to represent and act for them in the business of making laws.

The Senate.

Number. There are forty Senators, from thirty-nine senatorial districts. The Lieutenant-Governor is the presiding officer.

Elected. By the people; one-half being chosen every two years until the general election in 1907. At that time, and every four years thereafter, the entire senate will be chosen at one time for a term of four years.

Qualifications. A Senator must be an actual resident of the district for which he is elected; must be legally qualified to vote for members of the General Assembly; must hold no salaried office under the State government.

Powers. Shall select its own officers; choose from its own body, in the absence of the Lieutenant-Governor, or when he exercises the office of Governor, a president PRO TEMPORE; confirms or rejects nominations; has sole power to try impeachment.

SENATORIAL DISTRICTS are the districts into which a State is divided for the election of senators. There are thirty-nine districts in Virginia, and each of them elects one senator, except the district formed of Richmond and the County of Henrico, which elects two. PRESIDING OFFICER is a person who PRESIDES or acts as president or chairman in any assembly or meeting.

A candidate for the Senate must be LEGALLY QUALIFIED TO VOTE for members of the General Assembly. This means that he must be a citizen of the United States, a resident of Virginia for two years, and have the other legal qualifications of voters as required by the Constitution.

PRO TEMPORE is a Latin phrase meaning FOR THE TIME--that is, for a short time or temporarily. The Senate elects one of its own members to preside PRO TEMPORE if the lieutenant-governor happen to be absent, or when he is called upon to act as governor. (See under Powers and Duties of governor, page 28.) The Senate has the power to CONFIRM OR REJECT NOMINATIONS. Many public officers of the State are appointed by the governor, but when he nominates or NAMES a person for a public office he sends the nomination to the Senate, and it may confirm--that is, approve of--the nomination, or it may reject it. If it should reject the nomination, the person nominated is not appointed.

IMPEACHMENT means a charge of dishonesty or serious neglect of duty made against a public official. In an impeachment it is the House of Delegates which must make the charge and act as prosecutor, but it is the Senate which must try the case and pass sentence on the accused, if proved guilty.

House of Delegates.

Number. Composed of one hundred members apportioned by statute among the counties and cities of the State.

Elected. By the people for two years.

Qualifications. Same as for Senators.

Powers. Elects its own Speaker and all other officers; impeaches State officers, and prosecutes them before the Senate. The Clerk of the House of Delegates is also Keeper of the Rolls.

Apportioned means divided or distributed or allotted. A statute is any law, but the word is most commonly understood to mean a law made by a legislature representing the people. The number of delegates appointed to the counties and cities--that is, the number which each is entitled to elect--is decided by statute in proportion to the number of inhabitants.

The chairman of the House of Delegates is called the speaker. The same title is given to the presiding officer of the lower house in nearly every legislature in English-speaking countries.

The rolls are the statutes in written form as passed by the Assembly. A law when proposed in the Assembly is called a bill. To become a statute a bill must be voted on and have a majority three times in the House of Delegates and three times in the Senate and be signed by the governor. Then it is an act, or a Statute, or a law. The copy signed by the governor is an engrossed or written copy, and the official copies of the laws so engrossed are the rolls, and are preserved by the keeper of the rolls, who is the clerk of the House of Delegates.

General Assembly. (Senate and House jointly.)

Sessions. Biennial. Beginning the second Wednesday in January of every even year, and continuing sixty days. The session may be extended not exceeding thirty days. It may be convened in special session by the Governor.

The Senate and House of Delegates jointly--that is, both together --are called the General Assembly. Sessions means sittings or meetings for business, and biennial means happening once every two years. The General Assembly meets once every two years, and it does business for sixty days. If the business necessary to be done require more time, the session may be extended--that is, lengthened--thirty days. A special session is a session convened-- that is, called to meet--for some special or particular business. The governor may convene such a session whenever he thinks it necessary.

Powers. General powers of legislation under the constitution. Elects U. S. Senators, County and City Electoral Boards, Auditor of Public Accounts, Second Auditor, Register of the Land Office, Superintendent of Public Printing, the Judges of the Commonwealth; decides contests in the election of Governor and Lieutenant- Governor; confirms or rejects nominations of certain officers made by the Governor, the State Board of Education, etc.

Powers means what the General Assembly has power to do. Legislation is the making of laws. The Assembly has powers of general legislation under the constitution--that is, of making all such laws as the constitution directs or does not forbid. (Explanations are given later on as to the boards and officers mentioned here which the General Assembly has power to elect.)

Contests--that is, disputes or differences--may occur in the election of governor and lieutenant-governor. There may be contests as to counting of votes or as to the qualifications of candidates. Such contests are decided by the General Assembly.

Membership. Each house settles its own rules of proceeding; is judge of the election, qualification, and returns of its members. Members are not subject to arrest under any civil process during the session of the General Assembly, nor for fifteen days next before the convening, and after the termination of each session; are privileged from arrest in all cases during the session, except for treason, felony, perjury, breach of the peace, or a contempt of court of a criminal nature.

What is meant by each house being judge of the election, qualification, and returns of its members is, that it can decide whether the members are legally elected and qualified. Returns are the particulars as to names of candidates and the number of votes cast for each, which the election judges are required to make up after the close of the poll on election day. The qualifications necessary for a member of either house are as follows: he must be twenty-one years of age or over, and a voter of the State of Virginia, and he must reside in the district for which he is elected.

Civil process is a law-proceeding in a case where no crime is charged, but such as for the recovering of a debt or for the settlement of a difference relating to business matters. Perjury is the crime of wilfully making a false oath. When a person appears as a witness in a court of law he has to take an oath that he will tell the truth. If after taking such oath he tells what he knows to be untrue, he is guilty of perjury.

A breach of the peace is any act of violence which causes public disturbance, such as one person assaulting another and thereby causing a quarrel or riot.

Contempt of court is disobedience to the orders or decrees or rules of a court of law. Insult or violence to a judge in court would he criminal contempt.

Salaries. The President of the Senate and the Speaker of the House of Delegates, each, $400; and the other members, each, $240 for attendance and service at each regular session; at all extra sessions, the President of the Senate and Speaker of the House of Delegates shall receive, each, $240, and the other members, each, $120.

Members are entitled to mileage.

In addition to his salary each member of the Assembly receives ten cents per mile for expenses of traveling to and from the sessions of the Assembly. This allowance is called mileage.

Bills may originate in either of the two houses. No bill shall become a law until it has been read on three different days in each house except by a vote of four-fifths of the members voting in each house.

Every bill which shall have passed the Senate and House of Delegates shall, before it becomes a law, be presented to the Governor; if he approve, he shall sign it and it is then a law, but if not, he shall return it with his objections to the house in which it originated; who shall proceed to reconsider it. If after such consideration two-thirds of the members present shall agree to pass the bill, it shall be sent to the other house, by which it shall be reconsidered, and if approved by two-thirds of all the members present, it shall become a law, notwithstanding the objections of the Governor.

He may also veto any particular item of an appropriation bill, but this item may also be passed over his veto by a two-thirds vote of both houses.

If any bill shall not be returned by the Governor within five days after it shall have been presented to him, it shall be a law in like manner as if he had signed it.

A bill is a draft or statement of a proposed law. A bill may originate in either house--that is, it may be first proposed in either the Seriate or House of Delegates. Any senator or delegate who wishes to have a new law made must first put it in writing. Then he himself introduces or proposes it in the house of which he is a member, or it may be introduced by a committee.

A committee is a number of persons, usually not a large number, appointed by a legislature or other body to take charge of and attend to some particular business. The members of the House of Delegates and of the Senate are divided into committees, and some special subject or business is entrusted to each. For example, in the Senate there are committees on Privileges and Elections, Public Institutions and Education, and many other subjects; and in the House of Delegates there are committees on Courts of Justice, Schools and Colleges, and other subjects.

Usually proposals for new laws are referred for consideration to the committee having charge of the subject or business to which the proposed law relates. Committees in the Senate are elected by the senators themselves; committees in the House of Delegates are appointed by the speaker.

When a new law or bill is introduced it is either proposed by a committee, or by some member and given for consideration to a committee. In order to pass, it must be read three times on three different days (once each day) in the house in which it originates.

The first reading is the formal placing or presenting of the bill before the house. At the second reading the bill is discussed, and any member who wishes to say anything for or against it is at liberty to do so.

Amendments may also be proposed at the second reading. An amendment is an alteration or a change in the wording or matter of a bill. After an amendment is discussed the house votes upon it, and if a majority is for it, the change is made in the bill.

When all amendments are discussed and voted on, a vote is taken on the bill as a whole, and if a majority of the members vote for it, it is read a second time.

It is then engrossed, or written out, by the clerk of the house, and read a third time, after which a vote is again taken, and if there is a majority for it, it passes the house.

When the bill is passed in the house in which it originated, it is taken to the other house by the sergeant-at-arms. There it goes through the same forms of reading and discussion, and if it be read three times and have a majority in its favor it is passed. It is then enrolled, after which it is signed by the presiding officer in each house, and when this is done it is sent to the governor for his signature.

The sergeant-at-arms is an officer whose duty it is to preserve order in the chamber where the sessions of either house are held, to distribute among the members any papers or documents they may require, and in general to perform such services as are necessary for the proper transaction of business. Each house has its own sergeant-at-arms.

(For enrolling, see under House of Delegates, page 19.) The requirements with regard to a bill after it is sent to the governor are stated in the text above. (For the veto power of the governor, see page 28.)

QUESTIONS.
1. In whom is the legislative power of the commonwealth vested?
2. What is the legislative power?
3. Define commonwealth.
4. What is a delegate?
5. How many members constitute the Senate?
6. What are senatorial districts, and how many are there in the State?
7. Who is the presiding officer of the Senate?
8. For how long are senators elected?
9. What are the qualifications of a senator?
10. What are the powers of the Senate?
11. What does impeachment mean?
12. Who tries a case of impeachment?
13. How many members of the House of Delegates?
14. Define statute.
15. For how long are members of the House of Delegates elected?
16. What are the qualifications of delegates?
17. What are the powers of delegates?
18. Define apportioned.
19. What is the chairman of the House of Delegates called?
20. What are the rolls, and by whom are they kept?
21. What does the General Assembly consist of?
22. How often are the sessions of the General Assembly held?
23. What is a special session?
24. What are the powers of the General Assembly?
25. What officers does it elect?
26. What is legislation?
27. What are contests in elections of governor and lieutenant- governor, and who decides them?
28. What is meant by each house being judge of the election, qualifications, and returns of its members?
29. What are election returns?
30. Define civil process.

31. What is perjury?
32. What is contempt of court?
33. What are the salaries of the officers and members of the Assembly?
34. What is mileage?
35. What is a bill?
36. Tell how a bill becomes a law.
37. What is a committee?
38. Define amendment.

III.
EXECUTIVE DEPARTMENT.

Governor. Elected. By the people for four years. Must reside at the seat of government during his term of office; not eligible for the next succeeding term. Salary, $5,000 a year. He shall receive no other emolument from this or any other government.

The seat of government is the city or town in which the Legislature holds its sessions. Richmond is the seat of government of the State of Virginia. Term is the period of time for which a public officer is elected. The term of the governor is four years. He is not eligible--that is, he cannot be elected--for the next succeeding term--that is, he cannot be governor for two terms, one immediately following the other. Emolument is salary or compensation or pay.

Qualifications. Must be at least thirty years of age; must be a citizen of the United States; must have been for the five years next preceding his election a resident of the State. If of foreign birth, he must have been a citizen of the United States for the ten years next preceding his election.

Foreign birth means birth in any country outside the United States. But the children of American citizens are citizens of the United States, even though they have been born in another country.

Powers and Duties. The chief executive officer of the commonwealth; shall take care that the laws are faithfully executed; shall communicate to the General Assembly, at every session, the condition of the commonwealth, and recommend such measures as he may deem expedient; may call special sessions of the General Assembly; shall be Commander-in-Chief of the Land and Naval Forces of the State; may embody the militia to repel invasion, suppress insurrection, and enforce, the execution of the laws; shall conduct all intercourse with other and foreign states; may fill temporarily, during the recess of the General Assembly, all vacancies in those offices for which the constitution and laws make no provision; may remit fines and penalties, grant reprieves and pardons, remove political disabilities, and commute capital punishment; shall attest all commissions and grants; signs or vetoes bills passed by the General Assembly.

The governor is the chief executive officer. He is called chief because he is the highest public officer of the State, and executive because it is his duty to execute or carry out the laws. It is also his duty to send what is called a message to each session of the General Assembly. The message is a letter or statement in which he communicates to the Assembly full information as to the condition of the State, and recommends such measures--that is, such new laws--as he thinks necessary.

Militia is a body composed of citizens enrolled and trained as soldiers for the defence of the State. All able-bodied male persons between the ages of eighteen and forty-five years may be called to serve in the militia. Naval forces are military forces or militia that serve on sea.

Invasion is the entrance into a State of a military force from another country for the purpose of conquest. To repel invasion is to oppose it by force, to drive off the invaders. Insurrection is a rising or rebellion of people in a State against the government of their own State. It is the duty of the governor to suppress-- that is, to put down--insurrection, and to ENFORCE the EXECUTION of the laws--that is, to carry out the laws by force if necessary. INTERCOURSE is correspondence with others by letter or message. When it is necessary to have intercourse with another State or a foreign country, the governor, as the chief executive and highest representative of the people, is the person who conducts such correspondence.

The recess of the General Assembly is the time when it is not in session. During recess of the Assembly, the governor may fill vacancies in public offices for which the Constitution and laws make no provision. For example, the Constitution and laws make no provision for the appointment of judges during the recess of Assembly; therefore, if a judge dies during the recess, the governor appoints a person to fill the vacancy until the Assembly meets and elects a new judge.

A FINE is a PENALTY or punishment in the form of payment of money. Sometimes a person convicted of an offence against the law is ordered by the judge to pay a sum of money instead of being sent to jail. This is called a FINE. But it may happen that the person is convicted by mistake or by false evidence, or that the fine is too heavy for the person to pay. In such cases the governor may REMIT the FINES--that is, release or free the persons from having to pay.

The governor may also GRANT REPRIEVES AND PARDONS if he sees good reason for doing so. A reprieve is a delay of punishment. When a person is convicted of murder, the judge sentences him to be put to death on a certain day. But there may be reason for further inquiry into the case, and to give time for such inquiry the governor may postpone the execution of the sentence--that is, put it off to another day. This is called a reprieve. If the further inquiry should prove that the person is innocent, a full pardon is granted and the person is set free.

POLITICAL DISABILITIES are punishments which deprive persons of certain rights of citizenship. A citizen convicted of bribery in an election, embezzlement of public funds, treason, felony, or petit larceny, is by the law of Virginia deprived of the right of voting. This is a POLITICAL DISABILITY. The person convicted is legally DISABLED to vote. The governor may remove the disability, and this restores to the person his right of voting. The governor may also COMMUTE CAPITAL PUNISHMENT. To COMMUTE is to CHANGE, and CAPITAL PUNISHMENT is the punishment of DEATH--the punishment inflicted on persons convicted of murder. The governor may order that instead of being put to death the convict be imprisoned for life, or for a number of years. (A convict is a person CONVICTED or found guilty of crime.)

The governor shall ATTEST ALL COMMISSIONS AND GRANTS. To ATTEST is to certify, or bear witness to, and a COMMISSION is a written paper giving power or authority to some person or persons to perform a public duty. When a judge is elected he receives a commission authorizing him to act as such, and the governor attests the commission by signing his name to it. GRANTS or gifts, such as grants of public lands or money for educational or other public objects, are also made in writing, and must be attested by the governor. (Commissions and other important papers must have upon them an impression of the seal of the State. The seal is a circular piece of metal made like a medal or large coin and bearing on each side certain figures and mottoes. The impression of the seal shows that the paper has been officially attested or certified.)

The VETO power is one of the most important powers possessed by the governor. When a bill is passed by the General Assembly it is sent to the governor for his signature. If he SIGN it--that is, writes his name upon it--it is then a law. If he VETO the bill, or any item contained in it appropriating money, the bill, or such part of it as is vetoed, cannot become a law until it is again passed by a two-thirds vote of both houses. (VETO is a Latin word meaning I FORBID.)

In case the Governor dies, or is in any way incapacitated for performing the duties of his office, the Lieutenant-Governor shall act; and in case of the inability of both, the President PRO TEMPORE of the Senate shall act.

INCAPACITATED for office means legally disqualified. The governor would be incapacitated if he should refuse to qualify by taking the necessary oath, or if he should reside out of the State, or if he should be convicted on impeachment.

LIEUTENANT-GOVERNOR.

Elected. At the same time and for the same term as the Governor, and his qualifications and the manner of his election in all respects shall be the same.

He shall be the President of the Senate, but shall have no vote, except in case of an equal division.

For the same term means for the same length of time. The governor is elected for four years. That is his term of office. The term of the lieutenant-governor is the same.

An equal division is an equal number voting for and against the same proposal. If a bill is proposed in the Senate and twenty senators vote for and twenty against it, that is an equal division. In such case, and in no other case, the president votes. He may vote on either side he pleases, and his vote is called a casting vote.

ATTORNEY-GENERAL.

Elected. By the people for four years. Salary, $2,500 and mileage.

Duties. Shall give his opinion and advice when required to do so by the Governor, or by any of the public boards and officers at the seat of government; shall appear as counsel for the State in all cases in which the commonwealth is interested, depending in the Supreme Court of Appeals, the Supreme Court of the United States, the District and Circuit Courts of the United States for the State of Virginia, and shall discharge such other duties as may be imposed by the General Assembly. Member of the State Board of Education.

An attorney is a person who acts for and in the place of another. The word is usually applied to a lawyer who is employed by another to act for him in any law business he wishes to have done. An attorney who appears in a court of law and acts or defends a person, or acts against a person accused of crime, is called a counsel.

The attorney-general is a lawyer who is elected to do law business for the State. He must appear in court as counsel for the State in every case in which the commonwealth (meaning the whole people) is interested. The commonwealth is interested in every case of crime, because it is for the interest or well-being of the people that those who commit crime should be punished. If this were not done-- if criminals, persons who commit murder or burglary or theft--were not arrested and punished, no man's life or property would be safe. The attorney-general must appear and act for the commonwealth in any of the courts above mentioned whenever there is a case in any of them in which the people of the State are interested.

Depending or pending with reference to a case means that the case is in court waiting to be tried or decided. (For information as to Supreme Court of Appeals and Circuit Court of the City of Richmond, mentioned above, see under Judiciary Department.)

The Supreme Court of the United States is the highest court of the United States. Its members or judges are appointed by the President and hold office for life, and it sits at Washington and tries cases in which any person or persons are accused of violating the Constitution of the United States. The members of the district and circuit courts of the United States are also appointed by the President. These courts sit in various districts of States, and try cases in which persons are accused of violating the laws of the United States--that is, the laws made by Congress.

The word circuit means a going round. A district in which the same judges go round at certain times and hold courts in several places is called a circuit, and the courts so held are called circuit courts.

QUESTIONS.
1. For how many years and by whom is the governor elected?
2. Where must the governor reside?
3. Is the governor eligible for a second term?
4. What is the governor's salary?

5. What is the seat of government?
6. What qualifications are necessary in a candidate for governor?
7. Mention some of the powers and duties of the governor.
8. Why is the governor called the chief executive officer?
9. What is the governor's message?
10. What is the militia?
11. Define naval forces, invasion, insurrection.
12. What is a fine?
13. What is a reprieve?
14. What are political disabilities?
15. What is capital punishment?
16. Define commissions and grants.
17. What is the veto power?
18. When does the lieutenant-governor act as governor?
19. In case of the inability of both the governor and lieutenant- governor, who acts as governor?
20. How is the lieutenant-governor chosen?
21. What are the qualifications of the lieutenant-governor?
22. Does the lieutenant-governor ever vote in the Senate?
23. What is an equal division?
24. What is an attorney?
25. For how long is the attorney-general elected?
26. What is his salary?
27. What are his duties?
28. What are circuit courts?

IV.
EXECUTIVE DEPARTMENT--Continued.

Secretary of the Commonwealth.

Elected. By the people at the General Election for a term of four years. Salary, $2,500.

Duties. Shall keep a record of all executive acts; shall attest the signature of the Governor on all official documents; shall keep the seals of the commonwealth; shall arrange and preserve all records and papers belonging to the Executive Department; shall be charged with the clerical duties of that department, and render the Governor such services as he may require in the dispatch of executive business; shall be general librarian, and have charge of the library fund; shall receive and transmit election returns directed by law to be sent to him, and keep a record of the certified statements and determinations of the Board of State Canvassers; issue certificates of election; collect tax on State seal; keep on file the reports of other departments and make and record a summary of each; record all charters of incorporation; shall make quarterly reports to the Governor.

COMMISSIONS are fees or payments for certain work done. The secretary of the commonwealth may charge fees for making out copies of any public papers or documents kept hi his office, or for issuing commissions (letters of appointment) to certain public officers. The person who receives the copy or commission must pay the fee.

A RECORD is a written account or description of any business or work done. EXECUTIVE ACTS are official acts of the governor. The secretary of the commonwealth must make records of such acts and preserve them in his office. He must sign his own name after the signature of the governor on all official documents. This is called ATTESTING the signature.

There are two SEALS OF THE COMMONWEALTH. One is called the GREAT SEAL, and the other the LESSER SEAL. (For form and description of seal, see under POWERS AND DUTIES of governor, page 28.) The great seal is much larger in size than the lesser. It is affixed to documents signed by the governor which are to be used for purposes outside the jurisdiction of the State, or, for example, in a United States court, or in another State or foreign country. The lesser seal is affixed to public documents signed by the governor which are issued for use within the State.

CLERICAL DUTIES are the duties of writing letters, records, and other papers or documents. A GENERAL LIBRARIAN is one who has general charge or control of a library. The LIBRARY FUND is the books and maps belonging to the State. These are kept in the State library at the capital, and the secretary of the commonwealth is the librarian.

ELECTION RETURNS when made up by the judges of election are sent to the commissioners of elections and afterwards to the Board of State Canvassers. The board determines and decides who have been elected, and the secretary must KEEP A RECORD of the Board's DETERMINATIONS.

After the election returns are examined by the State board, the secretary makes out CERTIFICATES OF ELECTION for certain State officers elected at the polls. The certificate is a paper certifying or stating that the person has been elected. There is a TAX or charge on the use of the State seals on certain documents, and this tax is collected by the secretary of the commonwealth. The secretary must KEEP ON FILE--that is, preserve--in his office the reports of other public departments of the State, and make a summary, or sketch, of the contents of each.

A CHARTER OF INCORPORATION is a paper or document granted by the General Assembly, and giving power to a number of persons to carry on business as a corporation, or to the people of a town or city to carry on the business of government within their own districts.

TREASURER.

Elected. At the General Election for term of four years. Salary, $2,000 and commissions allowed by law.

Duties. Shall receive and disburse, only upon a warrant from the proper Auditor, all moneys paid into the Treasury of the State; shall pay interest on certain bonds as they become due and payable; shall be the custodian of bonds held by the

Commissioners of the Sinking Fund, and of bonds deposited by foreign express and insurance companies doing business in the State; shall make quarterly and annual reports to the Governor.

The treasurer is the person who receives and takes charge of money belonging to the State. The building in which the money is kept and in which the treasurer has his office is called the treasury. The treasurer also disburses money. To disburse is to pay out, and the treasurer cannot disburse without a warrant from the auditor (see next section).

The warrant is a writing giving the treasurer power to pay money. The treasurer pays the interest on State bonds. A bond is a written paper by which a person binds or pledges himself to pay a certain sum of money before a certain day. Sometimes the government has to borrow money, and when it does so it issues bonds to the persons who loan the money. In these bonds the government binds itself to pay the money by a certain time, and to pay a certain amount every year as interest until the principal (the full amount borrowed) is paid back.

The sinking fund is money set apart at certain times to pay the debts due by the government. It is in charge of officers called commissioners. These commissioners hold bonds for debts due to the government on account of the sale of public lands, and the interest of the State in railroads and other corporations. Express companies and insurance companies whose head-quarters are in foreign countries, and who do business in Virginia, are required to give bonds to the State as security that their obligations to citizens of the State shall be honestly carried out.

AUDITOR OF PUBLIC ACCOUNTS.

Elected. By the General Assembly for term of four years beginning on first day of March succeeding election. Salary, $4,000.

Duties. Shall audit all pecuniary claims against the commonwealth, except those chargeable to the Board of Education, Corporation Commission, or any corporation composed of officers of government, of the funds and property of which the State is sole owner; shall settle with officers charged with collecting the revenues of the State; shall issue warrants directing the Treasurer to receive money into the Treasury, and warrants upon the Treasurer in payment of all claims except those mentioned above; shall report to the Superintendent of Public Instruction by September 15th, in each year, ninety per cent, of the gross amount of funds applicable to public school purposes for the current year; shall make quarterly and annual reports to the Governor.

An auditor is a person who audits or examines accounts or statements of the receipt and expenditure of money, to see that they are correct.

Pecuniary claims are claims for the payment of money. Such claims made against the commonwealth are not paid until they are examined by the auditor of the public accounts. Claims that are chargeable --that is, to be charged--against the Board of Education, the Corporation Commission, or corporations of government officers, are not audited by the auditor of public accounts, but by the second auditor (see next section). To report ninety per cent, of the school funds is to state the amount to that extent that is ready to be apportioned or divided among the cities and counties for school use (see under sections Superintendent of Public Instruction and School Funds).

SECOND AUDITOR.

Elected. By the General Assembly for four years from the first of March next succeeding election. Salary, $1,700 and commissions allowed by law.

Duties. Shall register all coupon and registered bonds and fractional certificates issued on account of the public debt, and all bonds redeemed and cancelled by the Commissioners of the Sinking Fund; shall be the custodian of the books of the Commissioners of the Sinking Fund, and securities for money belonging thereto; shall audit all claims on account of the Board of Education, Corporation Commission, and any corporation composed of officers of government, of the funds and property of which the State is sole owner; shall issue his warrant for all moneys received into the Treasury, or drawn out of it on account of these boards and corporations, the Sinking Fund and the Literary Fund; shall make quarterly and annual reports to the Governor.

To register bonds is to enter particulars of them in books kept for the purpose. Coupon bonds are bonds with interest coupons or certificates attached to them, and bearing no name, but payable to any person who presents the coupons at the treasury at certain times. Registered bonds are bonds bearing the name of the person who receives them, and payable to that person or any person to whom he may sell or transfer them.

Fractional certificates are certificates or bonds issued for any fractional part of one hundred dollars of the public debt. All other bonds are issued for amounts of one hundred dollars or some multiple of a hundred.

A bond is redeemed--that is, bought back--when it is received at the treasury or office of the sinking fund and the amount of it is paid to the holder. The bond is then cancelled. To cancel is to deface or destroy so that the paper or bond cannot be used again.

A security is something given or deposited as a pledge that money loaned shall be repaid. Debts may be due to the sinking fund by railroad or other companies in which the State has an interest, and securities have to be given that such debts shall be paid.

The literary fund was formed in 1810 from the sale of public lands, some of which had been possessed by the Church in colonial times. The fund has since been increased by the sale of lands given to the State by Congress for public school purposes. and by fines collected for offences committed against the State, and by donations made by private individuals. It is called the literary fund because it is used for purposes of education.

Register of the Land Office.

Elected. By the General Assembly for a term of four years from the first of March next succeeding election. Salary, $1,800. He is also Superintendent of Public Buildings.

Duties. Shall issue grants to all purchasers of waste lands; record all grants and patents, and furnish lists to the clerks of the county and corporation courts; shall keep the records, documents, and entries of Northern Neck Lands, and of lands granted, or to be granted, by the Commonwealth; shall have care of the public buildings and all other public property at the seat of government not placed in charge of others; shall have control of Capitol Square; shall try, prove, and seal weights and measures; shall report semi-annually to the Auditor of Public Accounts.

The land office is the office in which business connected with the sale or granting of public lands is conducted. This business is under the control of an officer called the register of the land office, and public buildings in the State are under his care. He is also superintendent of weights and measures. At his office are kept weights and measures, provided by the State, to be furnished to counties and corporations as standards by which the weights and measures in business use throughout the State are tested. The State weights and measures are tried by the register once every ten years, and when proved to be correct are marked with a seal. In every county there is a sealer of weights and measures, who must examine, once every three years, the weights and measures in use throughout the county, to see that they are up to the standard.

A patent is a government paper granting to some person or persons the sole right to any lands, privileges, or inventions.

The Northern Neck was the name given in colonial times to the peninsula lying between the Rappahannock and Potomac Rivers.

State Corporation Commission.

Composed of three members appointed by the Governor, subject to confirmation by the General Assembly, for a term of six years each. Salary, $4,000 each.

At least one of the Commissioners must have the qualifications prescribed for judges of the Supreme Court of Appeals.

Duties. Shall issue all charters or amendments thereof for domestic corporations and licenses to do business in the State to foreign corporations; arrange for visitation, regulation and control of all corporations doing business in the State; prescribe the forms of all reports and collect and preserve such reports. Shall control all transportation companies; fix the amount of their taxes; prescribe rates, charges and classifications of traffic and enforce the same.

Has the powers and authority of a court of record to administer oaths and compel attendance of witnesses, and all appeals from the Commission shall be to the Supreme Court of Appeals only. Shall make annual reports to the governor.

The term corporation or company includes all trusts, associations and joint stock companies having any powers or privileges not possessed by individuals or unlimited partnerships. Charter means the charter of incorporation under which any such corporation is formed.

A transportation company is any company or person engaged in the business of a common carrier. A transmission company includes any company or person owning and operating a telephone or telegraph line for hire. Public service corporations include transportation and transmission companies, gas, electric light, heat and power companies and all persons authorized to use or occupy any street or public place in a manner not permitted to the general public.

Bonds are certificates of indebtedness issued by any corporation and secured by a mortgage or trust deed.

Domestic corporations are such as are chartered under the laws of Virginia. Foreign corporations are such as are incorporated under the laws of some other state or country.

The General Assembly may place under the control of the Corporation Commission divisions or bureaus of insurance, banking, etc.

Every domestic and foreign corporation doing business in the state shall file in the office of the Corporation Commission an annual report as prescribed by law setting forth various facts regarding its business, and organization, the names of its officers, its place of business and such other information as may be required by law.

A corporation may be established for the transaction of any lawful business or to promote or conduct any legitimate object or purpose.

Any number of persons not less than three may associate to incorporate a college, an alumni association, a literary society, a cemetery company or association, a fraternal benefit association, a fraternal association, society, order or lodge, a society for the prevention of cruelty to children or animals, a charitable or benevolent association, or social, hunting, fishing club, or any society, organization or association of a similar nature.

A corporation may be limited as to duration to the time stated in its charter. But when no time is so limited it shall be perpetual, subject to the power of repeal reserved to the General Assembly.

A corporation may sue and be sued in any court of law and equity.

With regard to railroads, canals, and all transportation and transmission companies, the State Corporation Commission has all the power and authority formerly belonging to the office of railroad commissioner; examines them as to their condition, the causes of accidents, etc.; requires changes and improvements; contracts with them for the conveyance of convicts, lunatics, etc.

Every railroad company in Virginia has a charter from the State, in which are stated certain conditions on which, in the interests of the people, they must carry on their business. It is the duty of the Commission to examine the railroads from time to time to see that they are operated in such a way that there shall be no danger to the people who travel upon them.

To contract is to make an arrangement or a bargain for some work to be done. The Commission makes contracts with the railway companies for carrying convicts to prison from the place in which they are tried and convicted, and for carrying lunatics to the asylum or hospital in which they are to be confined.

With regard to internal improvements in which the State is interested, the Commission has all the authority formerly exercised by the Board of Public Works; appoints State directors and State proxies for works in which the State is interested; keeps a register of all property belonging to the State; represents the State in relation to all corporations whether as a stockholder, creditor, mortgagor, or otherwise.

Internal improvements are public works of various kinds for the improvement of the State, such as railroads, canals, highways. Money of the State may be invested in the capital of corporations carrying on internal improvements, and it is the duty of the Corporation Commission to watch and protect the interests of the State in such undertakings.

For this purpose the Commission appoints directors and proxies to act in such companies. A proxy is a person appointed as a substitute for another. Proxies are appointed to represent and vote for the State at meetings of corporations for internal improvements, in which the State holds stock.

A TOLL is a charge made for passing certain canals, bridges, etc. The Commission has the power to fix the amount of toll when it is not specified in the charter of the canal or bridge company.

Superintendent of the Penitentiary.

Appointed. By the Board of Penitentiary Directors for term of four years. Salary, $1,600.

Duties. Shall reside at the Penitentiary and be its chief executive officer; shall have control and custody of the property of the Penitentiary; shall employ a guard; shall report quarterly to the Governor, and monthly and annually to the Board of Directors.

The PENITENTIARY is the State prison at Richmond in which persons convicted in the State courts are imprisoned.

The GUARD is a body of men employed at the prison by the superintendent to prevent prisoners from escaping and to suppress rebellion by the prisoners if attempted. The Board of Directors is the board or body of men who have the management of the penitentiary. They are also appointed by the governor.

Superintendent of Public Printing.

Elected. By the General Assembly for term of four years. Salary, $1,500.

Duties. Must be a practical printer; shall have the supervision and management of the public printing and binding of the Commonwealth; shall report annually to the Governor, and biennially to the General Assembly.

The numerous public departments and offices of the State require to have a great deal of printing done. The acts passed by the General Assembly, the reports of public boards and of public officers, and the proceedings and decisions of some of the courts have to be printed and bound into books. It is the duty of the superintendent of public printing to make contracts for such work and all other printing and binding required for State purposes, and to see that it is properly done.

Commissioner of Agriculture and Immigration.

Elected. By the people at the General Election for term of four years. Salary, $2,000.

Duties. Subject to the Board of Agriculture and Immigration, he shall be the executive officer of the Department; shall examine and test fertilizers, collect mining and manufacturing statistics, establish a museum of agricultural and horticultural products, woods and minerals of the State; shall investigate matters pertaining to agriculture, the cultivation of crops, and the prevention of injury to them; shall distribute seeds; shall disseminate such information relating to the soil, climate, natural resources, markets, and industries of the State as may attract capital and induce immigration.

It is the business of the Board of Agriculture and Immigration to promote the interests of farming throughout the State and to encourage the introduction of capital and immigrants into the State. The COMMISSIONER OF AGRICULTURE is its executive officer. STATISTICS are statements of facts, usually accompanied by figures, showing the condition or progress of countries or peoples or industries.

The MINING AND MANUFACTURING STATISTICS of the State tell how many mines and manufacturing establishments are open in the State, how much work they do, how many people they employ, and give other important information regarding them.

A CABINET OF MINERALS is a collection of specimens of minerals, such as coal, ores, and metals. The commissioner of agriculture must keep in his office a collection or cabinet of samples or specimens of the minerals of Virginia, and the place where they are kept must be open to the public.

He must also make arrangements for providing from foreign countries such farm seeds as he may think of value to the people of the State, and he must DISTRIBUTE them in a careful and judicious manner among the people.

Commissioners of the Sinking Fund.

Composed of the Treasurer, Auditor of Public Accounts, and the Second Auditor.

For explanation of the SINKING FUND, etc., see under Treasurer and Second Auditor, pages 34-36.

Board of State Canvassers.

Composed of the Governor, Secretary of the Commonwealth, Auditor of Public Accounts, Treasurer, and Attorney-General.

Duties. Shall examine the certified abstracts of votes on file in the office of the Secretary of the Commonwealth, and make statement of the whole number of votes given at any General State election for certain State executive officers and for members of the Senate and House of Delegates, Representatives in Congress, and electors of President and Vice-President of the United States, and determine what persons have been duly elected.

The manner of voting at elections is explained on page 14, and the duty of the secretary of the commonwealth with regard to election returns is explained on page 33. The election returns, made up after the close of the polls on election day, are sent to the office of the clerk of the county or corporation in which the election is held.

Election returns are the books containing the names of the candidates and the number of votes given for each. On the second day after the election the COMMISSIONERS OF ELECTION meet at the clerk's office and make out ABSTRACTS of the result of the voting and send them to the secretary of the commonwealth.

An abstract is a paper containing the name of the person or candidate who has received the highest number of votes, and the number of votes received. Abstracts are made out for governor and lieutenant-governor, for attorney-general, for secretary, for treasurer, for superintendent of public instruction, for commissioner of agriculture and immigration, for senators and delegates, for electors for President and Vice-President, for congressmen, and for county, district, and corporation officers voted for at the election. When the abstracts are made out they are certified and signed by the commissioners and attested by the clerk, who acts as clerk for the commissioners.

To CERTIFY is to state or declare that anything is true or correct. The commissioners certify the abstracts that they are correct, and they sign their names upon them. They are then CERTIFIED ABSTRACTS, and certified copies of the abstracts for State officers are sent to the secretary of the commonwealth. These abstracts are examined in the office of the secretary of the commonwealth, by the Board of State Canvassers, who determine who are elected.

The secretary of the commonwealth after recording the determinations of the commissioners makes out certificates of election for senators, delegates, congressmen, and State officers elected, except for the governor, lieutenant-governor, secretary, treasurer, and attorney-general. The certified abstracts of votes for these officers are transmitted to the speaker of the house of delegates by the secretary of the commonwealth, and the returns are opened and the votes counted and declared in the presence of the two houses of the general assembly within one week after the beginning of the session.

State Board of Education.

Superintendent of Public Instruction.

For the State Board of Education and the State Superintendent of Public Instruction, see under Education, Chapter XI.

QUESTIONS.
1. What is the term of office of the secretary of the commonwealth?
2. What is his salary?
3. Name some of his duties.
4. Define COMMISSIONS.
5. Define EXECUTIVE ACTS.
6. What are the seals of the commonwealth?
7. What is a certificate of election?
8. What is the term of office of the treasurer?

9. What is his salary?
10. What are his duties?
11. Define WARRANT; BOND.
12. What is the sinking fund?
13. What is the term of office of the auditor of public accounts?
14. What salary does he receive?
15. What are his duties?
16. What is the term of office of the second auditor?
17. What does REGISTERING BONDS mean?
18. What are coupon bonds? Registered bonds?
19. What are fractional certificates?
20. What does REDEEMING a bond mean?
21. What is the literary fund?
22. What is the term of office of the register of the land office?
23. What other offices does the register of the land office hold?
24. Mention some of the duties of the register of the land office.
25. What is the business of the land office?
26. What are the duties of the superintendent of weights and measures?
27. What is a patent?
28. What are the duties of the superintendent of the penitentiary?
29. What is the penitentiary?
30. What are the duties of the superintendent of public printing?
31. How is the commissioner of agriculture and immigration chosen and for how long?
32. What salary does he receive?
33. What is the business of the department of agriculture and immigration?
34. Define STATISTICS.
35. What do the mining and manufacturing statistics tell?
36. How many members constitute the State Corporation Commission?
37. How are they chosen?
88. What are their qualifications?
39. What are their duties?
40. What are internal improvements?

41. What are State depositaries?
42. What are the duties of State directors and proxies?
43. What are domestic corporations? 44. Define foreign corporations.
45. Who are the commissioners of the sinking fund?
46. What are the duties of the commissioners of the sinking fund.
47. What officers compose the Board of State Canvassers?
48. What are the duties of the Board of State Canvassers?

V.
JUDICIARY DEPARTMENT.

Supreme Court of Appeals.
Composed of five judges chosen by joint vote of the two houses of the General Assembly. Term, twelve years. Salary: President, $4,200; other judges, each $4,000. The judges shall not hold any other office or public trust; shall not practice law.

Qualifications of Judges. Must have held a judicial station in the United States, or have practiced law for five years.

Sessions. Shall hold a session annually at Richmond. Wytheville, and Staunton.

The Judiciary Department is that part of government which is administered by JUDGES. All the courts of law in the State in which judges sit and hear and decide cases, or all the judges of the State regarded as one body, may be called the JUDICIARY.

The highest court in the State is the Supreme Court of Appeals. It has five judges, who are elected by the General Assembly and hold office for twelve years. The five judges appoint one of their number to be PRESIDENT of the court, and they appoint or select another who must reside at the seat of government. While they hold office as judges of the Court of Appeals they are not allowed to PRACTICE LAW--that is, to act as attorney or counsel (see under Attorney-General, page 29).

JUDICIAL STATION is the station or rank or office of a judge. A person cannot be elected judge of the Supreme Court of Appeals unless he has previously been a judge in the United States, or has practiced law for five years.

The SESSION of the court is the number of days it sits for business at any one place and time.

Jurisdiction. Shall have original jurisdiction in cases of habeas corpus, mandamus, and prohibition; shall have appellate jurisdiction in all cases involving the constitutionality of a law with reference to the Constitution of the State or the United States, or involving the life or liberty of a person, and in other cases prescribed by law. Shall not have jurisdiction in civil cases where the amount in controversy, exclusive of costs, is less than $300, unless such controversy relates to the title or boundary of land; or the probate of a will; or the appointment or qualification of a personal representative, guardian, committee, or curator; or a mill, roadway, ferry, or landing; or the right of the state, county or municipal corporation to levy tolls or taxes; or involves the construction of a law, ordinance, or proceeding imposing taxes; and, except in cases of habeas corpus, mandamus, or prohibition, the constitutionality of a law, or some other matter not merely pecuniary.

JURISDICTION means the power of a judge or of a court of law. APPELLATE jurisdiction is the power of a court to hear and decide cases of APPEAL against the decisions of lower courts.

This is the principal business of the Supreme Court of Appeals. In trials in the lower courts it frequently happens that the judge gives a decision which some lawyer acting in the case may think is not in accordance with law, or is not fair to his client. Whenever this happens, the lawyer may take the case to the Supreme Court of Appeals and ask the judges there to set aside the decision of the judge in the lower court. In cases of appeal, the court in which the decision appealed against has been given is called the LOWER COURT, A person who employs a lawyer to act for him in any law business is called a CLIENT.

The Supreme Court, after hearing the complaint or appeal against the decision of the lower court, considers the case and gives judgment on the question. This judgment is final--that is, it ends the case--unless there is some point in the question which has to do with the Constitution of the United States.

A writ is a paper issued by a judge, or court, commanding some person or persons to do something, or to abstain from doing something. Habeas corpus is a Latin phrase meaning you may have the body. A writ of habeas corpus is an order from a court directed usually to a warden or keeper of a prison, and commanding him to bring some particular prisoner before the court so that it may be decided whether there is just cause for his detention.

A mandamus is an order from a superior court to any person, corporation, or inferior--that is, lower--court requiring them to do something which it is part of their duty to do. A writ of prohibition is an order from a superior court prohibiting an inferior court from hearing or deciding a case, on the ground that it (the inferior court) has no jurisdiction in such case.

When the amount in controversy between two parties is less than $300, exclusive of costs--that is, excluding or not counting costs--the case cannot be appealed to the Supreme Court. In such cases that court has no jurisdiction. The idea of this law is that for sums less than $300 it would be absurd to go to the Supreme Court, as the costs might be greater than the sum in dispute. But if the dispute be about the title or boundary of land, or any of the other matters mentioned in the remainder of the sentence, the case may go before the Supreme Court of Appeals, even though the sum mentioned in the case be less than $300.

The title of land is the right of ownership, and a paper certifying that a person is the owner of certain land is a title deed. The probate of a will is the proof or proving of a will. A will is a statement, generally in writing, in which a persons declares his will, or wish, as to how he desires his property to be disposed of after his death. Wills must be probated--that is, proved in the proper court--before they can be legally executed.

A personal representative is one who executes a will (carries out the directions contained in it) or administers the estate or property of a deceased person. A guardian in law is one appointed by a court to take charge of and administer the property of persons who are not of sufficient age or understanding to manage their own affairs. A committee in law is one entrusted with the care of an idiot or a lunatic. Used in this sense, the word is pronounced com-mit-tee. A curator is one appointed to act as guardian of the estate of a person not legally competent (qualified) to manage his property, or of the estate of an absentee.

To levy means to raise or collect. Each county in the State has the right to levy tolls and taxes to pay the cost of carrying on its government. The constitutionality of a law is its agreement with the Constitution. The Supreme Court of Appeals has the jurisdiction to decide, when appealed to, whether any law is constitutional or not--that is, whether or not it is allowed by the Constitution of the State of Virginia.

Circuit Courts.

There are twenty-four judicial circuits, with a judge for each circuit. The judge must reside in the circuit for which he is elected; shall not hold any other office or public trust; shall not practice law. Elected by the General Assembly for terms of eight years. Salary, $2,500, except the judge of the circuit which includes the city of Richmond, who receives $3,500. Circuit judges are entitled to mileage.

Terms. There shall be at least five terms in each county and two terms in each year in each city except in cities of the second class that have their own courts.

For explanation of circuits, see under Attorney-General, page 30.

The term of a court is its regular session, or sitting, for the hearing and trying of cases. The word court means not only the room or hall in which a judge sits to try cases, but it means the judge while sitting in court, or a number of judges sitting in court together. An order of the court means an order given officially by a judge.

Jurisdiction. Shall have original jurisdiction for the trial of all presentments, informations and indictments for felonies; of all cases in chancery and civil cases at law, except cases to recover personal property or money of less value than $20; of all cases for the recovery of fees, penalties, etc.; of questions regarding the validity of ordinances and by-laws of a corporation; or involving the right to levy taxes; and all cases civil or criminal when an appeal may be had to the Supreme Court of Appeals. Also, of all proceedings by quo warranto; and may issue writs of habeas corpus, mandamus, prohibition, and certiorari to all inferior tribunals; issue writs of mandamus in all matters arising from or appertaining to the action of the board of supervisors; determines the probate of wills and testamentary cases; may appoint guardians, curators, commissioners in chancery, etc.

Appellate jurisdiction of all cases, civil and criminal, where an appeal writ of error or supersedeas may be taken or allowed by said courts from or to the judgment or proceedings of an inferior tribunal. But no circuit court shall have any original or appellate jurisdiction in criminal cases arising within the territorial limits of any city wherein there is established by law a corporation or hustings court.

Original jurisdiction means jurisdiction from the beginning of a case--that is, power to take up and try it when it is first entered in law. The Supreme Court of Appeals has not this power. It can deal only with cases that have already been tried in some other court. But the circuit courts may try cases on their first hearing. This is original jurisdiction. They have also general jurisdiction--that is, they can try all cases in general in which the law is violated, or the protection of the law is sought or required.

A presentment is a notice taken by a grand jury of any offence or crime of which they may have knowledge. (For grand jury, see page 70.) The notice is a written statement of the facts, and the statement is sent or presented to the court in which the case may be tried.

After the presentment is made, the commonwealth's attorney prepares an indictment. This is a written charge against the accused person, with full particulars of the crime or offence alleged. The grand jury next make an investigation of the indictment by examining witnesses on oath, and if they think that the evidence is sufficient to prove the charge against the accused, they write on the indictment the words a true bill.

This does not mean that the person is found guilty, but that the grand jury find the case against the accused is so strong that it ought to be tried by a judge and jury, and so the person is brought into court and tried. But if the grand jury find that there is not evidence enough to convict the accused, they mark or indorse the indictment with the words not a true bill, and then there is no trial in court.

An information is an action or prosecution for some offence against the government, and it is based not on a grand jury indictment, but on a statement or complaint made on oath by a competent witness.

In chancery means in equity--that is, in natural right. A court of chancery may give a decision or judgment on the ground of plain, common justice between man and man, where there may be no statute law that bears upon the case. This is what is called equity. Personal property is movable property, such as furniture, money, etc. Immovable property, such as land or houses, is called real estate. Circuit courts have no jurisdiction for the recovering of personal property of value less than $20, the reason manifestly being that the cost of a circuit court trial of such a case might amount to a much greater sum than the sum in dispute.

The circuit courts have appellate jurisdiction in cases appealed from inferior tribunals--that is, lower courts. (For civil case, see under General Assembly, page 21.) A criminal case as distinguished from a civil case is one in which a person is charged with a crime or felony. A writ of error is an appeal ordered on the ground of an error or mistake in the proceedings of a court, either as to a matter of fact or a point of law. A supersedeas is a writ, or order, to suspend the powers of an officer, or to stay--that is, stop--action under another writ.

Quo warranto is a Latin phrase, the English of which is by what warrant or authority. In law it means a writ brought before a court to inquire by what authority a person or corporation exercises certain powers. For example, if a person assume the duties or work of a public office, and it is believed that he has no legal right to the office, proceedings in quo warranto may be taken against him.

Certiorari is a writ from a superior court in a certain case, ordering the removal of the case from an inferior court, so that more speedy justice may be obtained or that errors may be corrected. (For charters of incorporation, see under Secretary of the Commonwealth, page 33.) A receiver is a person appointed by a court to receive, or hold in trust, property about which law proceedings are being taken. Commissioners in chancery are commissioners or officers appointed from time to time by circuit court judges to examine and report upon accounts (statements relating to money) presented as evidence in the trial of a case.

Testamentary cases are cases about wills. A testament is a written paper in which a person declares (or testifies) how he wishes his property to be disposed of after his death. Such a paper is sometimes called a last will and testament. An injunction is an order of a court requiring a person to do or refrain from doing certain acts.

The Circuit Court of the City of Richmond possesses all the powers of other circuit courts except as to those matters the jurisdiction of which has been exclusively invested in the Chancery or the Hustings Court. It shall also have jurisdiction of all such suits, motions, prosecutions, and matters and things as are specially cognizable by it, in which the Commonwealth, represented by certain public officers or public boards, is a party.

The Circuit Court of the City of Richmond has the same power as other circuit courts except in matters the jurisdiction of which belongs EXCLUSIVELY to the Hustings Court, and the Chancery Court of the City of Richmond--that is, belongs to them and to no other court. (For explanation as to these matters, see under Hustings Court and under Chancery Court.)

A suit or lawsuit is an action or proceeding--in a court of law to recover a right, or to obtain justice in a matter under dispute. A suit at law is sometimes also called a cause. A motion (in law) is a carrying on of a suit or action in court to obtain some right, or to punish persons who have committed crime. Cognizable means liable to be taken notice of. Matters that are cognizable by a court are cases that it is fit and proper for it to hear, try, and decide.

A party to a suit is one of the two opposing persons or sides engaged in it. In every lawsuit there are at least two parties. The party or person that brings on the suit or action is called the plaintiff, because he makes a complaint or charge against some one; the party on the other side is called the defendant, because he defends himself against the charge.

QUESTIONS.
1. How many judges constitute the Supreme Court of Appeals?
2. How long is the term of each judge?
3. What salaries do they receive?
4. Do they hold any other office or practice law?
5. What are their qualifications?
6. Where are the sessions of the Supreme Court held?
7. Define judiciary.
8. Define judicial station.
9. What is a session of court?
10. Define jurisdiction.
11. What is appellate jurisdiction?
12. What is the principal business of the Supreme Court of Appeals?
13. What is a lower court?
14. What is a client?
15. When and how may an appeal be made from the judgment of the Supreme Court of Appeals?
16. In what other cases besides appeals has the Supreme Court jurisdiction?
17. Define habeas corpus, mandamus, prohibition, and writ.
18. What are the cases in which the Supreme Court has no jurisdiction?
19. What are costs?
20. Define title of land, and title deed.
21. What is meant by probating a will?
22. What is a will?

23. What is a personal representative?
24. What is a guardian?
25. What is a committee?
26. Define curator and levy.
27. What is meant by the constitutionality of a law?
28. How many judicial circuits are there?
29. Where must a circuit court judge reside?
30. Is a circuit court judge permitted to practice law?
31. What are the salaries of circuit court judges?
32. What are their qualifications?
33. What are the terms of circuit courts?
34. What does a term of court mean?
35. What is the meaning of the word court?
86. Name some of the kinds of cases in which the circuit courts have jurisdiction.
37. What do you understand by original jurisdiction and general jurisdiction?
38. Define chancery, personal property, and real estate.
39. What is a criminal case?
40. What is a writ of error?
41. What is a supersedeas?
42. Define quo warranto.
43. What is a certiorari?
44. Define trustee and receiver.
45. What are commissioners in chancery?
46. What are testamentary cases?
47. Define testament.
48. What is an injunction?
49. What are the powers of the Circuit Court of the City of Richmond?
50. What is a lawsuit?
51. What is a cause?
52. What is a motion?
53. Define cognizable, party to a suit, plantiff, defendant.

VI.
JUDICIARY DEPARTMENT-Continued.

Corporation or Hustings Courts.
Held in each city of the first-class by the city judge. Judge elected by the General Assembly in joint session for a term of eight years. Salary, not less than 12,000 $.

Qualifications of a judge. Same as those of judges of the Supreme Court of Appeals.

Terms. Held monthly, except that the July or August term may be omitted.

Jurisdiction. Within the territorial limits of the city, same as circuit courts have in the counties. Concurrently with the circuit courts they have jurisdiction over all offences committed in any county within one mile of the corporate limits of the city.

Corporation courts, or city courts, are courts whose jurisdiction lies within corporations or cities, and the judges are called city judges.

There is a corporation court in each city of the first class, and also in all cities of the second class in which it has not been by special election or otherwise merged into the circuit court. The Hustings Court of the city of Richmond has a peculiar and limited jurisdiction which is explained later in this chapter.

The city judges hold office for eight years. Their salaries in cities of the first class are fixed or specially provided by law at not less than $2,000, but any city may increase such salary, but such increase shall be paid entirely by the city.

Every city judge must hold a term or session every month except July or August, in either of which the court term may be omitted-- that is, not held.

Cities of the first class are such as contain more than 10,000 inhabitants. All other cities are termed cities of the second class.

The Constitution requires the maintenance of city or corporation courts in all cities of the first class, but provides for the discontinuance of independent city courts in all cities of the second class whenever the people vote in favor of their abolition.

Upon the abolition of the corporation court in any city of the second class, the circuit courts of the circuit in which the city is located will arrange to hold regular terms in such city the same as in cities of the first class.

Within their respective limits--that is, each in its own city-- the corporation courts have the same jurisdiction as the circuit courts. This means that they have power to try the same kind of offences as may be tried in the circuit courts.

JUSTICES' COURTS.

Held by a justice of the peace; in the cities, by the mayor or police justice.

The judge who sits in & justice's court is called a justice of the peace, or simply a justice, and sometimes a police justice. Justices' courts and police courts are the courts in which generally all offences and cases not of a serious nature are tried and disposed of. (See under Justices of the Peace and under Magisterial Districts. For mayor, see under Government of Cities and Towns.)

Jurisdiction. Debt, exclusive of interest, not exceeding $100; fines, damages, etc., not exceeding $20; have jurisdiction of certain cases of unlawful entry and detainer, detinue, and search; may allow bail in certain cases. Shall have concurrent jurisdiction with the County and Corporation Courts of the State in all cases of violations of the revenue laws of the State and of offences arising under certain provisions of the Code, and exclusive original jurisdiction for the trial of all other misdemeanor cases occurring within their jurisdiction.

A person charged with refusing to pay a debt may be brought before a justice's court if the debt, without interest, is not greater than $100, and the justice has power to decide the case. He has also power to try cases in which offenders may be punished by having to pay fines or damages of not more than $20.

DAMAGES means money paid to compensate for the injury or DAMAGE done to any person or person's property.

UNLAWFUL ENTRY is entering unlawfully upon lands belonging to another, and UNLAWFUL DETAINER means unlawful detaining or holding possession of lands or houses belonging to another.

DETINUE is an action in law in which a person seeks to get back property of his which is unlawfully held or DETAINED by another. In such cases the justice may issue a warrant for SEARCH for the property detained.

A WARRANT is a document or paper issued by a judge giving power or authority to a policeman, or other officer of the law, to arrest a criminal, or an offender, in order to have him brought to trial. A warrant issued authorizing an officer to search for property stolen or detained, is called a SEARCH WARRANT. BAIL is security given for the release of a person from prison. When a person is arrested and charged with a crime he may, if the crime be not a very serious one, be let out of prison and left at liberty until trial, if some one will give security or pledge for him that he will appear in court on the day appointed for the trial. If the amount required is small, the security is usually given in the shape of money, but if the amount is large, it is given in the shape of a bond called a BAIL-BOND.

The person giving the bail-bond must be one who owns real estate to the value of the amount of bail, and if the person to be tried does not appear for trial at the time appointed, the person who gives the bond may be required to pay the amount into court.

CONCURRENT jurisdiction is the same or equal jurisdiction. REVENUE is the income or money which the State or corporation receives in the shape of taxes. TAXES are the moneys collected by the State or by towns or cities for defraying the expenses of government. The owners of certain kinds of property have to pay taxes in proportion to the value of their property.

VIOLATION OF THE REVENUE LAWS is a violation of any of the laws made for the levying and collection of taxes. There is a tax upon the selling of certain articles, such as liquors and tobacco, and if a person sells such articles without paying the tax, it is a violation of the revenue laws.

A CODE is a collection of the laws of the State or country. The Code of Virginia is a book containing the statute laws of Virginia. A MISDEMEANOR is any crime less than a felony. (For FELONY, see page 13.)

Hustings Court of the City of Richmond.

Judge elected by the General Assembly for a term of eight years. Salary, $3,500.

Qualifications. Same as those of a Circuit Judge. Terms. Held monthly except the month of August.

HUSTINGS is the name given to a court formerly held in many cities of England, and applied specially to a court held within the City of London before the Lord Mayor and other magistrates.

Jurisdiction. Exclusive original jurisdiction of all presentments, indictments, and informations for offences committed within the corporate limits (except prosecutions against convicts in the penitentiary); concurrent jurisdiction of all presentments, indictments, and informations for offences committed within the space of one mile beyond the corporate limits on the north side of the James River, and to low-water mark on the south side of James River; concurrent jurisdiction with the Circuit Court of the City of Richmond of actions of forcible or unlawful entry and detainer; exclusive jurisdiction of all appeals from the judgments of the Police Justice's Court, all causes removable from said court, all proceedings for the condemnation of land or property for public use, all motions to correct erroneous assessments.

CORPORATE LIMITS are the limits or boundaries of the area over which the corporation has jurisdiction. Here the phrase means the boundaries of the city of Richmond.

PROSECUTIONS AGAINST CONVICTS are prosecutions against convicts (prisoners) for crimes committed within the prison. All such crimes are tried in the circuit court of the city of Richmond.

CAUSES REMOVABLE FROM SAID COURT (police justice's court) are cases that may at the request of the parties concerned be taken out of that court and tried in another court.

The CONDEMNATION of land or property for public use means the deciding by a proper authority (a court or judge) that certain lands must be given for such use. (See page 12.)

An ASSESSMENT is the valuing of property for the purpose of fixing a tax upon it. If any owner of property in Richmond thinks the valuation of his property too high, and that therefore the tax is too high, he may object to the assessment as ERRONEOUS and have a motion brought before the Hustings Court to have the assessment CORRECTED.

Chancery Court of the City of Richmond.

Judge elected by the General Assembly for term of eight years. Salary, $3,500.

Civil Government of Virginia 57

Qualifications. Same as those of a Circuit Judge.

Terms. Shall hold four terms each year; but shall always be open as a Court of Probate. For explanation of CHANCERY, see page 50, and for PROBATE, see page 48. Jurisdiction. Shall exercise, within the corporate limits, exclusive jurisdiction concerning the probate and recordation of wills, the appointment, qualification, and removal of fiduciaries, and the settlement of their accounts; the docketing of judgments; the recordation of deeds and such other papers as are authorized or required by law to be recorded; exclusive jurisdiction of all suits and proceedings in chancery cognizable by law in the Circuit Courts of the Commonwealth, except such as are specially cognizable by the Circuit Court of the City of Richmond, and any duty devolved, or any power or jurisdiction conferred by law on the Circuit Courts, unless otherwise expressly provided, except as to matters of common law and criminal jurisdiction.

The RECORDATION of wills is the recording of them in the court in which they are probated. (For PROBATE OF WILLS, see page 48.) FIDUCIARIES are trustees or persons appointed to hold property in trust for others. The DOCKETING OF JUDGMENTS is making summaries or brief statements of them for the purpose of record. A docket is a small piece of paper containing the heads or principal points of any writing or statement.

A JUDGMENT is a sentence or decision pronounced by a court, or a judge of a court, on any matter tried before it. A DEED is a written paper containing the terms of a contract, or the transfer of real estate by the owner to a purchaser. DEVOLVED means transferred from one person to another.

COMMON LAW is the title given to laws which have not originated in any statute, but derive their force and authority from having been in use for many centuries. The common law of England, upon which the common law of Virginia is based, includes customs of the people of such long standing that the courts took notice of them and gave them the force of law. Common law is the UNWRITTEN law; statute law consists of the laws enacted and recorded by legislatures.

Law and Equity Court of the City of Richmond.

Judge elected by the General Assembly for a term of eight years. Salary, $3,500.

Qualifications. Same as those of a Circuit Judge. Terms. Shall hold four terms each year, beginning the second Monday in February, May, September, and December, continuing as long as the business of the Court may require.

For EQUITY, see under Circuit Courts, page 50.

Jurisdiction. Shall exercise within the corporate limits original jurisdiction concurrent with the Chancery Court (except as to the probate and record of wills; the appointment and qualification of fiduciaries; the EX PARTE settlement of their accounts; the record of deeds and other papers authorized or required by law to be recorded). Shall have within the same limits original jurisdiction concurrent with the Circuit Court, except all such suits, motions, etc., as are specially cognizable by said Court;--has the same power as to bail, injunctions, etc., as the Circuit Court, and appeals from its decrees and judgments shall be taken and allowed as if from a Circuit Court. This Court has no criminal jurisdiction.

EX PARTE is a Latin phrase signifying from or on one side only. An ex parte hearing in court would be a hearing taken by one side or party in the absence of the other. An EX PARTE SETTLEMENT is settlement made on the application of one party without notice to the other.

QUESTIONS.

1. Where are corporation courts held?
2. What is the term of office of a corporation's court judge, and what salary does he receive?
3. What are the qualifications of a corporation's court judge?
4. How often are corporation courts held?
5. What is the jurisdiction of these courts?
6. How long do city judges hold office, and what salaries do they receive?
7. What does within their respective limits mean?
8. What is the judge who sits in a justice's court called?
9. What is the jurisdiction of justices' courts?
10. Define DAMAGES.
11. Define UNLAWFUL ENTRY.
12. What does unlawful detainer mean?
13. Define DETINUE.
14. Define WARRANT and SEARCH WARRANT.
15. What is a bail-bond?

16. What is concurrent jurisdiction?
17. What is revenue?
18. Define TARIFF.
19. What is the code?
20. What is a misdemeanor?
21. How long is the term of office of the judge of the Hustings Court of the City of Richmond, and what salary does he receive?
22. What are the qualifications of the judge of the Hustings Court?
23. How often are terms of this court held?
24. What are corporate limits?
25. What do you understand by prosecutions against convicts in the penitentiary?
26. What does condemnation of land mean?
27. What is an assessment?
28. What does correcting erroneous assessments mean?
29. For how long does the judge of the Chancery Court of the City of Richmond hold office, and what salary does he receive?
30. What are the qualifications of the judge of this court?
31. How often does the court meet?
32. Mention some classes of cases in which the Chancery Court has jurisdiction.
33. What does the recordation of wills mean?
34. What are fiduciaries?
35. What does docketing of judgments mean?
36. Define JUDGMENT.
37. What is common law?
38. For how long does a judge of the Law and Equity Court of the City of Richmond hold office, and what is his salary?
39. What are the qualifications of a judge of this court?
40. How often and for how long does the Equity Court sit?
41. Tell of the jurisdiction of this court.
42. What does ex parte mean?
43. What is an ex parte settlement?

VII.
OFFICERS OF COURTS.

Clerks.

In all Justices' Courts, the justices are required to make and preserve their own dockets. The Clerk of the Court of Appeals is appointed by the court; the Clerks of the Circuit and Corporation Courts are elected by the people of the county or corporation in which the court is held. They hold office for a term of eight years. Salary, fees and special allowances.

Duties. Shall record the proceedings of their respective courts and issue writs in their name; shall be the custodians of all papers lawfully returned to or filed in the Clerk's office; shall perform such other duties as are imposed upon them by law.

The Tipstaff and Crier are the executive officers of the Court of Appeals.

For meaning of DOCKET, see under Chancery Court of the City of Richmond. DOCKETS here mean entries in a book giving lists of names of persons connected with the cases tried, and particulars of the proceedings in each case. In justices' courts such dockets are made and kept by the justice himself.

The clerks of the courts mentioned have no salaries. They are paid by fees and special allowances. For example, when a clerk of court makes out a writ or bond or a copy of any court document, he gets a fee for doing it. (See under Secretary of the Commonwealth, page 32.) A special allowance is an allowance (or a grant of money) made by the court for special work done.

The TIPSTAFF and CRIER are executive officers of the Court of Appeals--that is, they execute or carry out certain orders of the court. In some places a sheriff's officer is called a tipstaff, the name being derived from the custom of such officers bearing a STAFF TIPPED with metal.

Criers sometimes are appointed for other courts besides the Court of Appeals.

The name is derived from the practice of proclaiming or CRYING out in court the commands or orders of the judge.

Sheriff.

The Sheriff is the executive officer of the Circuit Court, and of the Circuit and Chancery Courts of the city of Richmond; the City Sergeant is the executive officer of the Corporation Courts and Circuit Courts held for cities, and the Hustings Court for the city of Richmond; the Constable is the executive officer of the Justice's Court.

Though the sheriff is an officer of the courts, he is more particularly a county officer. His principal duties will, therefore, be found set forth and explained under County Officers (see page 74). The city sergeant is also a court officer, but his duties are limited to cities. They are stated and explained under Government of Cities and Towns. The duties of the constable, who is a magisterial district officer, are explained under District Organization.

Commonwealth's Attorney.

Elected by the people at the general election in November for a term of four years; must reside in the county or corporation for which he is elected; shall hold no other elective office. Salary, allowance by the Board of Supervisors and fees.

Duties. Gives legal advice to the county and district officers, and prosecutes criminals in the Circuit and Corporation Courts.

For Board of Supervisors, see page 82.

LEGAL ADVICE is advice on matters of law. The commonwealth's attorney prosecutes criminals--that is, he attends in court and makes the charge, or states the case, and examines witnesses, against persons charged with crime.

A WITNESS is a person who tells on oath, in answer to questions, what he knows about the crime charged against the accused, or about the facts in a civil case or process. (See civil process and perjury, page 21.)

Attorney-at-Law.

Must hold license granted by any three or more judges of the Supreme Court of Appeals acting together under such rules and regulations and upon such examination both as to learning and character as may be prescribed by the said Court; must be a male citizen over the age of twenty-one years; must have resided in the State six months preceding application for a license; and must qualify before the Court in which he proposes to practice.

An ATTORNEY-AT-LAW is a person legally qualified and licensed to act as attorney. A person not a lawyer might be called an attorney if appointed to do any business on behalf of another, but to be an attorney-at law a person must be qualified as stated in the text. (See under Attorney-General, page 29.) A LICENSE is a permission to perform certain acts. It is usually in writing, and is issued by persons having legal authority to do so.

An attorney-at-law must QUALIFY before the court in which he wishes to practice. This means that he must produce evidence that he is legally licensed, that he must take an oath that he will perform his duties as an attorney, and also that he must take an oath that he will be faithful to the Commonwealth of Virginia.

Who May Practice Law in Virginia.

Any person duly authorized and practicing as Counsel or Attorney- at-Law in any State or Territory of the United

States, or in the District of Columbia; but if he resides in Virginia he must pay the prescribed license fee.

DULY AUTHORIZED means having received the proper license, and having qualified. PRESCRIBED LICENSE FEE is a certain fee or charge for the issuing of a license to practice in Virginia.

Juries.

Drawn by lot from a list of those well qualified to serve as jurors, furnished by the Judge of the Circuit or Corporation Courts. The list shall contain not less than one hundred nor more than three hundred names.

All male citizens over twenty-one years of age who have been residents of the State for two years, and of the county, city, or town in which they reside for one year next preceding their being summoned to serve as such and competent in other respects, are WELL QUALIFIED to SERVE as jurors within the State. But certain persons are disqualified as not competent, such as idiots, lunatics, and persons convicted of bribery, perjury, embezzlement of public funds, treason, felony or petit larceny.

Certain public officers and persons belonging to certain professions are exempt from jury service. The governor, the lieutenant-governor, postmasters, practicing physicians (doctors), and many others, are exempt from the duty of serving on juries.

Juries in civil and misdemeanor cases are chosen by lot. Once every year the judge of each circuit and corporation court makes out a list containing the names of not less than one hundred and not more than three hundred persons resident in the county or corporation and well qualified to serve as jurors. These names are written on slips of paper or ballots (each name on a separate ballot) and the ballots, after being folded so that the names may not be seen, are put into a box kept for the purpose by the clerk of the court.

Ten days before any term of a court at which a jury may be required, the clerk draws sixteen ballots from the box, without looking at the names until they are all drawn out. The persons whose names are thus drawn are summoned to attend at the term of court. Should more than sixteen be required, more are summoned, and on the day they attend the court their names are written on ballots and placed in a box, and from them the juries for the trial of cases are drawn in the manner already stated. This is what is called choosing or selecting BY LOT, the word lot meaning chance. It is considered the fairest way of forming a jury.

If jurors were appointed instead of being selected by lot, persons having prejudice or ill feeling against one of the parties in the case might be put on the jury, and the verdict rendered by such jury might be a very unjust one. But when the selection is by lot nobody knows who is to be on it, and so it is equally fair to both sides.

The number of persons on a jury is usually twelve, but in a civil case, if both parties consent, there may be a jury of only seven; or, the case may be tried and decided by a jury of three persons, one selected by each of the two parties to the suit, and the third by the other two; or, by the judge without a jury.

For juries in cases of felony the names of twenty persons residing at a distance from the place where the crime or offence is said to have been committed are taken from a list furnished by the circuit or the corporation court. Those twenty are summoned to attend the court, and from them a jury panel of sixteen is selected. The accused person may, without giving any reason, object to, or strike off, any four of the sixteen, and the remaining twelve will be the jury to try the case.

If the accused does not strike off any, or strikes off less than four, a jury of twelve is selected from the panel by lot. The attorney for the commonwealth--that is, the attorney who prosecutes the accused--may CHALLENGE--that is, object to--

-a juror, but he must assign a reason for his objection, and if the judge decides in favor of his objection, the person challenged is not put on the jury. A panel is a list of persons summoned to serve as jurors.

To SUMMON is to call or notify a person or persons to appear in court. A person who is summoned to attend as a juror and who, without sufficient reason, fails or neglects to do so, may be punished by a fine of not less than five nor more than twenty dollars.

Persons summoned as jurors are entitled to receive one dollar per day for service on a jury, and mileage at the rate of four cents per mile travelled in going to and returning from court. (Further explanation as to the duties of juries will be found under Petit Jury, page 71.)

Grand Jury.

Consists of not less than nine nor more than twelve persons taken from a list of forty-eight selected by the Judge of the Circuit or Corporation Court from the qualified jurors of the county or city in which his Court is held. A Special Grand Jury shall consist of not less than six nor more than nine persons.

The principal duties of the GRAND JURY are mentioned under Circuit Courts, page 55. The law requires that "the grand jury shall inquire of and present all felonies, misdemeanors, and violations of penal [criminal] laws committed within the jurisdiction of the respective courts wherein they are sworn."

To PRESENT is to make a statement or PRESENTMENT to the court as explained on page 55. Every grand jury has a chairman or speaker, who is appointed by the court and is called the FOREMAN. The foreman is required to take an oath or swear that he will "present no person through prejudice or ill-will, nor leave any unpresented through fear or favor," but that in all presentments he "shall present the truth, the whole truth and nothing but the truth."

In this way the foreman is SWORN, and the other grand jurors must swear that they will "observe and keep" the same oath taken by the foreman. An oath is a solemn statement or declaration with an appeal to God, or calling God to witness that what is stated is true or that the person shall tell the truth.

Witnesses before giving evidence in courts at the trial of a case must make oath or swear to "tell the truth, the whole truth and nothing but the truth." While the witness is repeating the words of the oath he holds a Bible or Testament in his hand,

and kisses it when he has repeated the words.

There are two kinds of grand juries--regular and special. There is a regular grand jury at two terms in each year, of the circuit, corporation, or hustings court. But a grand jury may be ordered by a circuit, corporation, or hustings court at any time there may be special or urgent need for it, and such grand jury is called a SPECIAL grand jury.

Grand jurors are entitled to the same compensation and mileage as petit jurors (see next section).

Petit Jury.

Consists of twelve members.

Duties. Hear evidence before the court in civil and criminal cases and render a verdict according to the law and evidence.

The PETIT JURY is the jury impanelled--that is, put on a panel or list--to try cases in court. How such a jury is formed is stated under Juries (see page 68). Petit jurors, like grand jurors, must take an oath to do their duty honestly. (The word jury is derived from the Latin word jurare, which means to swear.)

It is the duty of the petit jury to hear the evidence in the case it is to try, and to give a verdict in accordance with that evidence. If the evidence presented before the court proves the accused to be guilty, the jury must give a verdict of "guilty"; if the evidence is not sufficient to show that he is guilty, they must give a verdict of "not guilty." (For verdict, see page 11.)

The verdict of the jury must also be ACCORDING TO LAW. This means that the jury must give heed to the law of the case as explained by the judge. Evidence might be offered which would not be lawful. It is the duty of the judge to decide whether evidence is lawful or not, and if he decides that any evidence is illegal or unlawful, then the jury must not pay any regard to it in considering their verdict.

QUESTIONS.

1. By whom are court clerks appointed or elected, and for how long do they hold office?
2. How are court clerks paid? 8. What are the duties of court clerks?
4. What are dockets?
5. What are the tipstaff and crier, and what are their duties?

6. How is the commonwealth's attorney chosen, and for how long?
7. Where must the commonwealth's attorney reside, and how is he paid?
8. What are his duties?
9. What is LEGAL ADVICE?
10. What does prosecuting criminals mean?
11. What is a WITNESS?
12. What are the qualifications of an attorney-at-law?
13. Define LICENSE and QUALIFY.
14. Who may practice law in Virginia?
15. Define DULY AUTHORIZED and PRESCRIBED LICENSE FEE.
16. What are the qualifications of jurors?
17. What classes of persons are exempt from jury service?
18. How are juries in civil and misdemeanor cases chosen?
19. Describe the system of choosing or selecting by lot.
20. How many persons constitute a jury?
21. How are juries in cases of felony chosen?
22. What do you understand by CHALLENGING a juror?
23. What does SUMMON mean?
24. What does a grand jury consist of?
25. What is a special grand jury?
26. What are the duties of grand jurors?
27. What does PRESENT mean?
28. What is the duty of the foreman of the grand jury?
29. What is an oath?
30. How many kinds of grand juries are there?
31. What is the compensation of grand jurors?
32. What does a PETIT JURY consist of?
33. What are the duties of a petit jury?
34. What do you understand by rendering a verdict according to the law and evidence?

VIII.
COUNTY ORGANIZATION.

Counties.
Organized by the General Assembly under the provisions of the Constitution.
Objects. Convenience in administering justice and transacting local business.

Each county shall maintain at the county seat a court-house, clerk's office, and jail.

Counties are organized--that is, formed and invested with powers of government--by the General Assembly. The Assembly may form new counties out of other counties or parts of other counties, but the Constitution of Virginia directs that "no new county shall be formed with an area of less than six hundred square miles," and that the county or counties from which a new one is formed shall not be reduced below an area of six hundred square miles.

The convenience of having the State divided into counties may easily be seen. If there were no counties most of the people would have to go long distances to the State capital in order to have important business attended to. County organization brings the advantages of government and the administration of justice nearer the homes of all the people.

The COUNTY SEAT is the chief town of the county, where the public business of the county is chiefly transacted. The court-house is the building in which judges sit for the trial of cases. The jail of the county is the prison in which persons convicted of minor (trifling) offences are detained for punishment, and in which persons charged with serious crimes are held in custody until trial. Persons after trial and conviction for serious crimes are sent to the penitentiary.

COUNTY OFFICERS.

They are the executive officers under the authority of the laws of the State.

Sheriff.

Elected by the people for four years. Salary, allowance by the Board of Supervisors and fees.

Duties. Appoints his deputies; makes arrests; serves notices; collects fines; calls for troops in time of danger; executes any order, warrant, or process, lawfully directed to him, within his own county, or upon any bay, river, or creek adjoining thereto; levies on property and sells to satisfy order of court; attends the sittings of Circuit Courts; attends the meetings of the Board of Supervisors, and performs such duties as may be necessary for the proper despatch of business; must not practice law in any court of which he is an officer; cannot hold any other elective office; must give notice of violations of penal laws.

The salary or allowance for sheriffs is not the same in all counties, but varies according to the number of the population. It is paid by the Board of Supervisors. (For Board of Supervisors, see page 82.)

The sheriff may appoint deputies or assistants to help him in his duties, which are numerous and important. He is the principal executive officer of the county. It is his business to execute the judgments of the courts. If a person is sentenced to death, it is the sheriff who must make and direct the arrangements for carrying out the sentence.

A SENTENCE (in law) is the judgment, or declaration of punishment, pronounced by a judge upon a criminal after being found guilty. The sheriff must arrest and convey to prison any person or persons who have committed crime. He must serve legal notices, such as notices of decrees or judgments to be given against parties in cases of action for debt. He must collect fines that are not paid in court.

An important duty of the sheriff is to suppress riots or public disturbances, and if he finds that he and his officers are unable to do so, he may call upon the governor for troops (soldiers) to assist him. In such case the governor may send State militia to suppress the disturbance. The sheriff has charge or control of the county jail and the prisoners confined in it, and he must protect the prison and prisoners against violence or attack by mobs.

The sheriff must carry out any order or warrant or process of the courts. A

PROCESS is a summons or notice requiring a person to appear in court on a certain day to answer a charge to be made against him. If a court gives judgment against a person for debt or fine or taxes not paid, the sheriff LEVIES on the property of the person--that is, he takes or seizes it--and sells it to satisfy or execute the order of court.

It is also the duty of the sheriff to give notice to the attorney for the commonwealth of any crime (violation of penal laws) of which he may have knowledge. The sheriff cannot hold any other elective office--that is, an office to which a person is elected-- and he cannot act as a lawyer in any court for which he does duty as sheriff.

Commonwealth's Attorney.

See under Officers of Courts.

County Clerk.

Also Clerk of the Circuit Court elected by the people for term of eight years.

Duties. See under Officers of Courts.

A clerk of the county or a clerk of a court is an officer who does writing of various kinds, such as keeping records of public business, records of court proceedings, making out writs or bonds, or copies of court papers or documents. Many of the duties of clerks of counties and courts are mentioned in previous sections.

Treasurer.

Elected by the people for four years. Salary, commissions.

Duties. Shall receive the State revenues and the county (or city) levies, and account for and pay over the same as provided by law; shall keep his office at the county seat; shall receive taxes from July 1st to December 1st; after that add five per cent. and collect; shall settle with the Auditor of Public Accounts by December 15th, final settlement June 15th; may be required to make monthly settlements; in cities of Richmond, Lynchburg, and Petersburg, shall make weekly settlements; may distrain for taxes; shall post delinquent list; must reside in the county; shall not hold any other elective office; shall not own any warrant against the county or city; shall not lend out any public money, or use it for any purpose other than such as is provided by law; shall report violations of the revenue laws. Must reside in the county or city for which he is elected.

The STATE REVENUES are the taxes received for the State; the COUNTY

LEVIES are the taxes levied--that is, raised or collected-- for county purposes. These moneys the State treasurer must pay over as the law provides--that is, directs. The money collected for the county he must pay out for various public purposes relating to the county, but before making such payments he must have a warrant (written authority to pay) from the Board of Supervisors. The money he receives for the State he must pay to the auditor of public accounts.

The time for the receiving of taxes is from July 1st to December 1st each year. An addition of five per cent. is made to taxes not paid by the latter date. The treasurer must SETTLE with the auditor by December 15th--that is, he must by that time have paid over to him all moneys received for the State. By June 15th he must make a final settlement This means that he must settle for all taxes paid to him since December 15th, and furnish lists of those who have failed to pay. Besides county treasurers there are city treasurers. (See also under Government of Cities and Towns)

If any person fail or refuse to pay taxes assessed upon him, the treasurer may DISTRAIN his property to recover the amount. To distrain is to seize property for debt due. (To ASSESS is to fix or name a certain amount as a tax on property, or to value property with the object of fixing a tax upon it) A person who fails or neglects or refuses to pay his taxes is called a DELINQUENT, a word that means one who fails to perform his duty.

A DELINQUENT LIST is a list or paper containing the names of persons who have failed to pay the taxes, and a notice that at a certain time certain property of such persons will be sold if the taxes are not previously paid. A copy of the delinquent list must be posted at public places within the city or county in which the property to be sold is situated. A county treasurer is not himself allowed to purchase or own any warrant or claim against the county treasury. (A warrant here means an order for the payment of money.)

The REVENUE LAWS are the laws relating to assessing, payment, and collection of taxes. To conceal property so as to escape assessment of taxes, or to carry on certain kinds of business without paying the license or tax on such business, would be to violate the revenue laws. The treasurer must report all violations of the revenue laws of which he may have knowledge.

The salary of the treasurer is paid by commissions--that is, allowances--by way of percentages on the amounts he receives. The commission varies from two per cent, (two dollars for every hundred dollars) on large amounts, to three and five per cent, on small receipts.

Commissioner of the Revenue.

Elected by the people for four years; must reside in the district for which he is elected. Salary, commissions and fees.

Duties. Shall ascertain and assess, when not otherwise assessed, all the property, real and personal, not exempt from taxation, in his county, district, or city, and the person to whom the same is chargeable with taxes, all subjects of taxation, and also all male persons of full age and sound mind residing therein; shall issue licenses; register births and deaths; and report violations of the revenue and penal laws.

To ASCERTAIN all the property, real and personal, and the person to whom it is chargeable with taxes, is to find out where and what the property is and who is the owner, so that the proper tax may be assessed and charged against him. (For meaning of REAL and PERSONAL property, see under Circuit Courts, page 50.)

SUBJECTS OF TAXATION means property on which taxes may be charged or assessed. Certain kinds of property are exempt--that is, free-- from taxation in Virginia. All real estate or buildings owned by religious bodies and used as churches for divine worship are exempt from taxation. Public burying-grounds (cemeteries), real estate belonging to counties, cities, or towns, real estate belonging to the University of Virginia and other institutions devoted to purposes of education, real estate belonging to various benevolent institutions, such as lunatic asylums and orphan asylums, and in general all real estate devoted to religious, charitable, or educational uses, and not for profit to private individuals, are exempt from taxation.

A LICENSE is a permission or authority to carry on certain kinds of business or certain professions. Attorneys-at-law, doctors, dentists, and persons who manufacture or sell liquors, owners of theaters, and public shows, and people who engage in many other sorts of business must have licenses.

The licenses are issued or given out by commissioners of the revenue, and a certain sum must be paid for each, the money received being part of the public income or revenue for paying the expenses of government. Licenses are granted for a certain time. Many are granted for a year, and some for only a number of months or weeks or days. When the time specified in the license (which is a written or printed paper) expires, a new license must be obtained and another payment made.

It is the duty of the commissioner of the revenue to register (record) the births and deaths in his district. At the time that he ascertains the personal property in his district which is to be taxed, he must ascertain the births and deaths that have occurred during the past year, and enter or write the particulars in books kept by him for the purpose. He must write the name and date of birth of every child, and the name, address, and occupation of the father; and he must enter the name and place of birth, and the names of the parents, of any person who has died.

It is also the duty of the commissioner of revenue to report to the commonwealth's attorney any violation of the revenue or penal laws of which he may have knowledge.

The number of commissioners of revenue is not the same in all the counties. A great many of the counties have four each, and some have less. In counties having more than one, each commissioner has a district for himself.

Superintendent of the Poor.

Appointed by the Circuit Judge, on the recommendation of the Board of Supervisors, for a term of four years; must reside in the county or city for which he is elected. Salary, not to exceed $400.

Duties. Shall have charge of the Poor-house, receive and care for the paupers sent to him by the Overseers of the Poor; receive and disburse, under the direction of the Board of Supervisors, the poor levy; make an annual report to the Board of Supervisors.

In every county there is a POOR-HOUSE, usually having a farm annexed, and in it paupers are received and cared for at the public expense. A. PAUPER is a poor person who has no means of living and is supported in a public or charitable institution. (For OVERSEER OF THE POOR, see under District Organization.)

The POOR LEVY is the tax annually levied for the support of the poor-house. This levy is made by the Board of Supervisors (which see), and the amount collected is received and DISBURSED--that is, expended--by the superintendent of the poor for the purpose for which it is intended.

The superintendent must make a report annually to the Board of Supervisors. This means that he must make a statement for the board once every year, showing the number of paupers provided for during the year, giving the name of each and how long supported, and also showing the total amount of money expended, the work done on the farm, the crops raised, and other information and particulars relating to the management of the institution.

The salary of superintendents of the poor is not the same in all counties. It varies according to the population.

County Surveyor.

Appointed by the Circuit Court, on the recommendation of the Board of Supervisors, for four years; must reside in the county for which he is appointed. Salary, fees and mileage.

Duties. Shall promptly make surveys of land ordered by courts, and return true plat and certificate thereof; establish meridian line; locate land warrants.

A SURVEYOR is one who measures portions of land to ascertain their area, or who ascertains or fixes the boundaries, form, extent and position of any district or territory.

The COUNTY SURVEYOR must survey lands when ordered by the court, and make out and certify a TRUE PLAT of such lands. A PLAT is a plan or map or chart.

A MERIDIAN LINE, as meant in the text, is a line located at some central and easily reached place in the county, running due north and south for not less than three hundred yards, and marked at each end of the three hundred yards upon a solid stone fixed in the earth. This line is necessary for various purposes of surveying and map making. There must be a meridian line marked in every county, and when a new county is formed it is the duty of the surveyor to establish a meridian line.

TO LOCATE LAND WARRANTS is to lay off (mark out) and survey portions of waste land belonging to the State for persons who have purchased any of such land. The warrants or orders for the land are issued by the register of the land office on receipt of the purchase money (see page 37).

Superintendent of Public Schools. See Education.

County Board of School Commissioners.

See Education.

Electoral Board. Appointed by the Circuit or Corporation Court for term of three years; composed of three qualified voters, residents of the county or city. Salary, $2 for each day of actual service, not to exceed $10 a year.

Duties. Appoint for each election district of the county or city a registrar, who shall be a discreet citizen and resident of the election district, and who shall serve for two years; shall provide for new registration when necessary; shall appoint each year three competent citizens who are qualified voters, and who can read and write, to be judges of election for all elections in their respective election districts; shall designate five of the judges of election to act as commissioners, who shall meet at the Clerk's Office, open the election returns and ascertain from them the persons elected.

There is an Electoral Board for each county and city. As the duties of the board may be performed in a few days each year, the total salary for each member is limited to $10 a year.

AN ELECTION DISTRICT is constituted (made up) of a magisterial district in a county, and a WARD in a city. For the former, see MAGISTERIAL DISTRICTS. For WARD, see under GOVERNMENT OF CITIES AND TOWNS.

A REGISTRAR is an officer who registers or enters in books kept for the purpose the names of all persons in his district who are entitled to vote. He must be at his voting place on the second Tuesday in each year to register all qualified voters who shall apply to be registered, and ten days previous to the November elections he must sit one day to amend, and correct the list where necessary, and to register qualified voters not previously registered.

JUDGES OF ELECTION have already been mentioned and some of their duties explained. (See page 14, also under Secretary of the Commonwealth, page 32, and under Board of State Canvassers, page 43, for manner of receiving and dealing with election returns)

Board of Supervisors.

Composed of the Supervisors of the several magisterial districts of the county. Salary, $3 per day and mileage. The County Clerk is the clerk of the Board.

Duties. Shall audit the accounts of the county, and issue warrants in payment of claims; shall settle with the county officers, and take the necessary steps to secure a satisfactory exhibit and settlement of the affairs of the county; examine the books of the Commissioner of the Revenue; fix and order county levies and capitation tax; raise money for county expenses; represent the county; have the care of the county property and the management of the business and concerns of the county in all cases not otherwise provided for.

For SUPERVISORS OF MAGISTERIAL DISTRICTS, see under DISTRICT ORGANIZATION.

THE ACCOUNTS OF THE COUNTY are the statements of public moneys received and expended by county officers. All such statements must be audited by the Board of Supervisors. An EXHIBIT is a paper showing or proving the correctness of money accounts, such as a voucher or a receipt. A CAPITATION tax is a tax on persons (from Latin caput, the head). A capitation tax is levied on all male persons over the age of twenty-one. The Board of Supervisors represents the county in all public matters, as in any action at law taken for or against the county, and it has the care and control generally of the public property, and the direction of the public business affairs of the county.

Assessors.

Appointed for a term of four years; number same as the number of Commissioners of the Revenue; must be a resident of the district for which he is appointed. Salary, $2 for each day he is necessarily employed.

Duties. Examine, immediately after appointment, all the lands and lots, with the improvements thereon, within their respective counties, districts, and corporations, and ascertain and assess the cash value thereof.

The land within the districts is valued by the assessors with the object of fixing upon each property the tax to be levied. When the assessor of a district has completed his valuations and made a record of them, he must send a copy of the record to the auditor of public accounts, another to the commissioner of revenue for the district, and another must be filed and preserved in the office of the county clerk.

Coroner.

Appointed by the Governor upon the recommendation of the Circuit Court. A Justice of the Peace may act as Coroner. Salary, fees.

Duties. To hold inquest over the dead bodies of those supposed to have been killed by violence; may act as sheriff in certain cases.

Every county must have at least one CORONER, but a county may have more than one, if the circuit court thinks it necessary. In such case the court recommends the appointment of a second coroner and nominates two persons for the office. The governor appoints one of them.

The business of the CORONER is to hold an INQUEST or inquiry into every case of death supposed to have been caused by violence. The coroner's inquest is conducted much after the manner of a jury trial. There is a jury of six persons, summoned by the sheriff or sergeant or constable, and sworn "to diligently inquire, and true presentment make, when, how, and by what means the person came by his death."

After witnesses have been examined and the whole case has been thoroughly investigated, the jury gives its verdict. If the jury should find that murder or assault was committed on the deceased, and should charge any person with the crime, the coroner issues his warrant for the arrest of the person, and if found he is arrested and held in prison until he is tried by a judge and jury.

QUESTIONS.
1. By whom are counties organized?
2. What is the advantage of a division of a State into counties?
3. What institutions must each county maintain?
4. What is the COUNTY SEAT?
5. What are county officers?
6. For how long is the sheriff elected, and how is he paid?
7. Mention some of the duties of the sheriff.
8. What is a SENTENCE?
9. Define PROCESS and LEVIES.
10. What are the duties of the county clerk?
11. What is the term of the treasurer, and how is he paid?
12. Name some of the duties of the treasurer.
13. What are the STATE REVENUES?
14. How does the treasurer dispose of the moneys he receives?
15. What do you understand by a DELINQUENT LIST?
16. What are the revenue laws?
17. For how long is the commissioner of the revenue elected?
18. How is he paid?
19. What do you understand by ASCERTAINING all the property, real and personal?
20. What does SUBJECTS OF TAXATION mean?

21. What is a license?
22. What are the duties of the commissioner of the revenue regarding births and deaths?
23 By whom is the superintendent of the poor appointed?
24. What is his term of office?
25. What are the duties of the superintendent of the poor?
26 Where are the poor received and cared for?
27. Define PAUPER, POOR LEVY, and DISBURSED.
28. What does the annual report of the superintendent of the poor tell?
29. How is the county surveyor appointed, and how paid?
30. Mention some of the duties of the county surveyor.
31. Define SURVEYOR.
32. What is a plat?
33. What is a meridian line?
34. What do you understand by LOCATING LAND WARRANTS?
35. By whom is the Electoral Board chosen, and for how long?
36. What is the board composed of, and what remuneration do its members receive?
37. What are the duties of the Electoral Board?
38. What is an electoral district?
39. What is a registrar, arid what are his duties?
40. Of whom is the Board of Supervisors composed?
41. What salary do the members of this board receive?
42. Who is clerk of the board?
43. What are the duties of the Board of Supervisors?
44. What are the accounts of the county?
45. What is an exhibit?
46. What is a capitation tax?
47. Who appoints the assessors?
48. How many assessors are there, and what salary do they receive?
49. What are the duties of the assessors?
50. By whom is the coroner appointed, and how is he paid?
51. What are the duties of the coroner?

52 What do you understand by an inquest?
53. Tell how an inquest is conducted.

IX.
DISTRICT ORGANIZATION.

Magisterial Districts.

Each county shall be divided into as many compactly located magisterial districts as are necessary, not less than three.

There must be at least three and not more than eleven magisterial districts in each county, and in each district there must be one supervisor, three justices of peace, one constable, and one overseer of the poor.

Supervisor.

Elected by the people for four years; must be a resident of the district.

Duties. A member of the Board of Supervisors; shall inspect the roads and bridges in his district.

The general duties of the Board of Supervisors have been already explained, but each supervisor has special duties in his own district. He must inspect the public roads and bridges in his district twice every year to see that they are kept in repair, and he must once a year make a written report to the Board of Supervisors as to their condition.

For the time he is actually employed in such service each supervisor receives two dollars a day, paid out of the public funds of his own district, but he is not allowed for such service more than thirty dollars in any one year.

Justices of the Peace.

Three in each district; elected by the people for four years; must reside in the district. Salary, fees.

Duties. Is a conservator of the peace; must see that the laws are obeyed; may issue warrants, attachments, etc.; may hold court for the trial of causes. (See Justices' Courts.)

The jurisdiction of justices is fully explained under JUSTICES' COURTS. Justices of the peace receive no salaries, but they are allowed fees for the issuing and certifying of several kinds of legal documents.

A CONSERVATOR of the peace is a preserver of the peace. To preserve the peace is one of the chief duties of a justice of the peace, hence the title of his office. If he have good reason to believe that any person intends to commit an offence against another, it is the duty of a justice to issue a warrant for the arrest of such person, and to require him to give bail or security for his good behavior.

In general it is the duty of the justice of the peace to do everything necessary to prevent, as well as to punish, violations of the criminal law in his district.

An ATTACHMENT is a writ directing an officer of the law to arrest and bring into court a person who has been summoned to attend as a witness or a juror, but has failed to appear at the proper time.

Constable.

Elected by the people for four years; must reside in the district. Salary, fees.

Duties. To make arrests; to serve notices; to execute any order, warrant, or process, legally directed to him; attend Justices' Courts; execute its judgments, levy attachments, collect fines, report violations of the penal laws; may act as sheriff in certain cases.

The constable performs in his district the same sort of duties generally that the sheriff performs for the county.

Overseer of the Poor.

Elected by the people for four years; must reside in the district. Salary, $2 for each day actually engaged, but not to exceed $20 per year.

Duties. Shall care for and assist persons unable to maintain themselves, who have a legal settlement in his district; shall remove those not having a legal settlement; shall prevent persons from going about begging; may hold and administer certain property donated to charitable purposes; may place in an asylum, or bind out as an apprentice, any minor found begging, or likely to become chargeable to the county.

A LEGAL SETTLEMENT in the case of a pauper is residence for one year in the district and three years in the State. Paupers not having a legal settlement may be removed to the place where they were last legally settled, but a warrant of removal must be obtained from a justice of the county or district.

A MINOR is a boy or girl under twenty-one years of age.

Conservators of the Peace.

Every judge throughout the State; every justice, commissioner in chancery, and notary within his county or corporation; conductors of railroad trains on their trains; depot agents at their places of business; masters of all steamers navigating the waters of the State on their respective vessels.

A NOTARY, or notary public, is an officer who attests or certifies deeds and other papers, under his official seal. Statements in writing that require to be attested for business or legal purposes are usually taken to a notary to be signed by him after the party has made oath that the statements are true.

Conductors of railroad trains may arrest any persons who violate the peace on their trains, and keep such persons in custody until they can be given over to the proper authorities for trial. Railroad depot agents may do the same at their depots, and the masters or captains of steamers may do the same on their vessels while sailing in the waters within the State. This is what is meant by being CONSERVATORS of the peace. Judges have the same power throughout the State, and justices, commissioners in chancery, and notaries within their districts.

SCHOOL DISTRICTS.

Each magisterial district is also a school district, for which see under Education, page 99.

SCHOOL TRUSTEES.

One school trustee is appointed annually for each school district; see page 99.

DISTRICT BOARD OF SCHOOL TRUSTEES.

This board is composed of three trustees of the district; for its duties, see page 99.

QUESTIONS.
1. How many magisterial districts is a county divided into?
2. For how long is the supervisor elected?
3 What are the duties of a supervisor?
4. How many justices of the peace are elected for a district?
5 What are the duties of a justice of the peace?

6. What is a conservator of the peace?
7. What is an attachment?
8. For how long is a constable elected?
9. What are the duties of the constable?
10. For how long is the overseer of the poor elected?
11. What remuneration does he receive?
12. Name some of his duties.
13. What is a legal settlement?
14. What is a minor?
15. Who are conservators of the peace?
16. What is a notary?
17. What provisions with regard to schools are mentioned as being made in the magisterial districts?

X.
GOVERNMENT OF CITIES AND TOWNS.

A City is an incorporated community containing within well-defined boundaries five thousand or more inhabitants.

A Town is an incorporated community of less than five thousand inhabitants.

A Council includes any body or bodies authorized to make ordinances for the government of a city or town.

An incorporated town or city is a community chartered as a corporation, for explanation of which, see page 14.

Ordinances are laws made by the council of a city or town for managing the public affairs of the city, or town.

COUNCIL.

In towns it is composed of the Mayor and six Councilmen, elected every two years by the people of the town on the second Tuesday in June. The Mayor and each Councilman have the power and authority of a justice in civil matters within the corporate limits, and in criminal matters within these limits and one mile beyond them; may issue processes, and may hear and determine prosecutions, etc. In cities the Councilmen of each ward are elected by the people of such ward. The Council of cities of over ten thousand inhabitants is made up of two branches:--the Board of Aldermen and the Common Council, all of whom are elected for four years, one-half being chosen every two years. These provisions may be modified by the city charter. Members of Common Council shall hold no other office in cities; no city officer shall hold a seat in the General Assembly.

It is the aim of the Constitution that, so far as possible, all cities shall be organized under general laws.

A city charter is the law under which the city is governed. It is passed by the General Assembly, and it makes the city a corporation. It states what powers the corporation may exercise and what officers it may appoint or elect to carry on its government.

A charter is for a city what a constitution is for a State. It prescribes the system under which the city is to be governed.

The powers of the mayor and the councilmen as justices are modified--that is, regulated--by the city charter, so that they may not be exactly the same in all cities.

Cities are divided into districts called wards, and each ward elects a certain number of councilmen.

POWERS. To levy taxes; create corporate debt; impose tax on licenses; enact ordinances, and prescribe fines or other punishment for the violation thereof; appoint a collector of taxes, and other officers; disburse all money collected or received for the corporation; lay off and keep in order streets and public grounds; provide necessary buildings, a fire department, water works, cemeteries, etc.; abate nuisances; establish election districts; alter and rearrange wards; provide for weighing articles of merchandise; judge of the election, qualification, and returns of its own members; protect the property of the city, and preserve peace and good order therein.

To create corporate debt is to borrow money for carrying out purposes of city government. Charters of cities give power to borrow money for such purposes.

A nuisance is anything that is annoying or offensive, or dangerous to the health of citizens.

The council may provide in various parts of the city public weighing machines for weighing articles of merchandise purchased by citizens who may wish to ascertain whether they have got honest weight.

To protect the property of the city and to preserve peace and order is the most important business of the council. For this purpose it has power to organize and maintain a police force.

Mayor of City.

Elected by the people of the city for a term of four years; presides over the Council; and his powers and duties may be modified by the city charter.

Duties. The chief executive officer of the city; shall see that the duties of the various city officers are faithfully performed; may suspend for cause all town or city officers.

To suspend an officer is to remove him from his office for a time until any charge made against him of neglect of duty is investigated and decided on.

City Sergeant.

Elected by the people for four years.

Duties. Shall perform the duties, etc., prescribed by the city charter; and shall also within the jurisdiction of the courts of his city exercise the same powers, perform the same duties, and be subject to the same liabilities as the sheriff of a county; in towns he shall have the same powers and discharge the same duties as constables, within the corporate limits and for one mile beyond them; shall be the executive officer of the Corporation Court.

LIABILITY means responsibility. Sheriffs are responsible or answerable for the performance of their duties, and if they fail to perform them they may be fined or imprisoned. City sergeants are under the same liabilities.

CITY CLERK.

Elected by the people for eight years. See under Officers of Court.

COMMISSIONER OF THE REVENUE.

Elected by the people for four years. See County Organization.

COMMONWEALTH'S ATTORNEY.

Elected by the people for four years. See County Organization.

TREASURER.

Elected by the people for four years. See County Organization.

SHERIFF OF RICHMOND CITY.

Elected by the people for four years.

Duties. Shall attend the Circuit and Chancery Courts, and act as their executive officer; shall exercise the same powers, perform the same duties, have the same fees and compensation therefor, and be subject to the same penalties touching all processes issued by said courts, or by the clerks thereof, or otherwise lawfully directed to him, that the sheriff of a county exercises, performs, and is entitled or subject to in his county.

CITY SUPERINTENDENTS OF SCHOOLS.

Superintendents of Schools for cities are appointed by the State Board of Education. See under Education, page

QUESTIONS.
1. Define city, town, council.
3. What are ordinances?
8. Of whom is the council composed?
4. What is the term of office of a member of council?
5. What are the powers of the council?
6. How are the Councilmen in cities elected?
7. In cities of over ten thousand inhabitants how is the Council made up?
8. Of whom is the Common Council composed?
9. Are members of this body permitted to hold any other office?
10. What is a city charter?
11. What do you understand by the powers of the mayor and the councilmen as justices being modified?
12. What are wards?
13. Name some of the powers of the council.
14. What does creating corporate debt mean?
15. What is a nuisance?
16. What is the most important business of the council?
17. How is the mayor of a city chosen, and what is his term of office?
18. What are the mayor's duties?
19. What does suspending an officer mean?
20. How is the city sergeant chosen, and what is his term of office?
21. Name some of his duties.
22. What does liability mean?
23. What is the term of office of the commissioner of the revenue, the commonwealth's attorney, and the treasurer?
24. How long does the sheriff of Richmond City hold office?
25. Name some of his duties.
26. Who appoints superintendents of schools for cities?

XI.
EDUCATION.
STATE.-BOARD OF EDUCATION.

Composed of the Governor, Superintendent of Public Instruction, Attorney-General, three experienced educators elected from the faculties of certain State institutions, one City Superintendent of Schools, and one County Superintendent of Schools. These eight constitute the State Board of Education, and their several powers and duties as members of the Board are identical except that the two division superintendents shall not participate in the appointment of any public school official.

This Board shall have the management and investment of school funds; make by-laws for its own government, and for carrying into effect the school laws; audit claims payable out of State funds; arrange for summer normal schools of teachers for instruction in processes of school organization, discipline, and management; select text-books and educational appliances for use in the public schools of the State; appoint (and remove), subject to confirmation by the Senate, all county and city superintendents, and regulate all matters arising in the practical administration of the school system not otherwise provided for.

The three State officers are ex officio members of the Board. The three experienced educators are elected quadrennially by the Senate from a list of eligibles consisting of one from each of the faculties and nominated by the respective boards of visitors or trustees of the University of Virginia, the Virginia Military Institute, the Virginia Polytechnic Institute, the State Female Normal School at Danville, the School for the Deaf and Blind, and also of the College of William and Mary so long as the State continues its annual appropriation to the last-named institution. The city and county superintendents are selected by the other six members for terms of two years each.

School funds are moneys set apart or provided for the support of schools. In Virginia, school funds are provided by the State, the counties, and the districts (see under School Funds).

By-laws are laws or rules made by any association for the management of its affairs. The Board of Education makes by-laws for its own government and for administering the laws relating to the schools.

Claims payable out of State funds are claims which by law are to be paid out of the State funds. Such claims must be audited by the Board of Education. The salaries and expenses of State education officers are paid out of the State fund, and portions of the fund are divided among the counties and cities for the support of schools.

By arranging for meetings of teachers for instruction in the processes of school organization, discipline, and instruction, the State Board of Education does much to improve the schools of the State, and the great yearly institutes are of the highest value to the schools.

One of the most important duties of the State Board is in connection with the selection of text-books and the approval of educational appliances for the equipment of schools.

The general duties of the State Board of Education consist in regulating all matters arising in the practical administration of the school system not otherwise provided for. Uniformity of practice throughout the schools of the State is of the greatest importance, and the State Board wisely secures this by keeping in constant correspondence with officers and teachers throughout the system.

The State Board of Education chooses its own secretary, who is entrusted with many important duties in carrying out the plans and work of the board.

As all division superintendents are appointees of the State Board, it is provided in the Constitution that the two who are members of the State Board shall not participate in the election of school officers.

SUPERINTENDENT OF PUBLIC INSTRUCTION.

Elected by the people of the State for four years; salary, $2,000, and necessary traveling expenses; shall have his office at the capital; shall be the chief executive of the public free school system; shall determine the true intent and meaning of the school laws; shall receive reports from school officers; inspect schools, and decide appeals from the decisions of county superintendents; apportion State funds among the counties and cities of the State.

The public free school system is the system under which, as required by the law of Virginia, the public schools are free to all persons between the ages of five and twenty-one years residing within the school districts.

The superintendent of public instruction is the chief executive officer of the system, and when any dispute arises among school officers as to the meaning or application of school laws, it is his duty to determine--that is, to decide--it.

The superintendent of public instruction is also to a large extent a judicial officer, and his decisions as to the true intent and meaning of the school laws have very nearly as much force as the decisions of the courts.

The reports received from school officers by the State superintendent are embodied in his report made every two years to the governor, and by him transmitted to the General Assembly.

This report, in addition to the information received from the county and city superintendents, contains a large amount of statistics and reports in regard to private schools, colleges, and other institutions which are more or less under the care and subject to the control of the State.

COUNTY.--COUNTY AND CITY SUPERINTENDENTS.

Term, four years, beginning July 1st after appointment; must reside in the county or city for which he is elected, and shall hold no elective office; shall explain the school system, examine teachers and grant certificates, promote the improvement and efficiency of teachers, advise with and counsel trustees and teachers, visit and examine schools under his care and inquire into whatever concerns their usefulness and perfection; decide appeals and complaints; administer oaths and take testimony; apportion the school funds among the districts.

The county and city superintendents must hold examinations at certain times in their counties or cities to examine persons desiring to become teachers, and if, after examination, such persons are found qualified, they receive certificates as teachers.

In any case of appeal or complaint against any person connected with the schools in their districts the county or city superintendents must hold inquiry into the matter and give decision upon it. In making such inquiry they can call witnesses and administer oaths to such witnesses before taking their testimony.

It is also the duty of the superintendents to prepare annually a scheme or plan for apportioning the State and county school funds among the school districts under their supervision.

SCHOOL TRUSTEE ELECTORAL BOARD.

Composed of the County Superintendent of Schools, the Commonwealth's Attorney, and a resident qualified voter, not a county or state officer, to be appointed by the Judge of the Circuit Court; shall fill all vacancies in the district boards of school trustees. In cities and towns school trustees are appointed by municipal councils.

A vacancy occurs every year in each district board. The district board when first formed was composed of three members, one to serve three years, one to serve two years, and the other to serve one year, all appointments afterwards to be for three years each. Thus there is one vacancy every year in the board, and it is the duty of the School Trustee Electoral Board to appoint a new trustee to fill the vacancy.

County School Board.

Composed of the County Superintendent (who is ex officio president) and the District School Trustees of the county--"a body corporate"; shall make necessary bylaws and regulations, shall have a regular annual meeting between the 1st and 15th of August; shall prepare and file with the Superintendent before July 15th an estimate of the amount of money that will be needed for public school purposes in the county for the next year, also a similar list for each school district based on the estimate of the District Board, which lists the Superintendent shall lay before the Board of Supervisors; shall make settlement with treasurers and school officers; shall administer certain properties devoted to school purposes.

Ex officio is a Latin phrase meaning by virtue of office. The county superintendent is president of the County School Board, not by election or appointment, but because of his office as county superintendent.

A body corporate is a corporation, the meaning of which term is explained on page 14.

Property of any kind, either public funds or donations from private persons, set apart or devoted to school purposes in the county is administered by the County School Board--that is, managed and used by the board for the support of schools in the county.

District.--School Districts.

Each county shall be divided into compactly located school districts, which shall correspond with the magisterial districts, unless specially subdivided; except that a town of five hundred or more inhabitants may form a separate school district.

School Trustees.

One shall be appointed annually for each district for a term of three years; must be able to read and write.

School trustees are appointed annually by the School Trustee Electoral Board, as explained above.

District Board of School Trustees.

"A body corporate"--composed of the three trustees of the district; shall hold and manage the school property of the district; provide suitable school houses, etc.; enforce school laws; employ and dismiss teachers; suspend and dismiss pupils; see that census of children of school age (5 to 21) is taken every five years; submit to the County School Board annually an estimate of the amount of money needed for public school purposes in the district for the next scholastic year.

In cities the Board is composed of all the trustees in the city, and its duties and powers are modified and enlarged.

The census of children is the numbering or counting of the children residing in the district.

The scholastic year is the part of the year during which the schools are open.

The District Board of School Trustees has the whole care and administration of the schools in its charge, and is thus the most important local body in the civil government of the State.

School Funds.

1. State Funds. The interest on the literary fund, the capitation tax, and a tax on property of one mill on the dollar.

2. County Funds. Such tax as the Board of Supervisors may levy for county school purposes; fines and penalties imposed on the Superintendent; donations, or the income arising therefrom.

3. District Funds. Such tax as the Board of Supervisors may levy for the purposes of the school district; fines and penalties imposed on district school officers and teachers; donations, or income arising therefrom.

The County or City Treasurer receives and pays out all school funds.

For explanation of literary fund, see page 37, and for capitation tax, see page 82. The tax of one mill on the dollar means a tax of one mill on each dollar of the assessed valuation of the property.

Certain fines and other money penalties may be imposed by the Board of Education or by the courts or county superintendents for failing or refusing to perform certain duties Such fines and penalties are added to the school fund for the county

When district school officers or teachers are fined for neglect of duty the money goes to the district fund. Donations are contributions or gifts from private individuals. If such gifts are real estate, the income arising therefrom is the rent of such real estate or the interest on the amount realized by its sale.

Teachers.

Must hold a certificate of qualification in full force, issued or approved by the Superintendent of Schools of the county or city within which he proposes to teach.

The law requires that a teacher must be at least eighteen years of age. If the teacher has the necessary education to pass the required examination, a certain maturity is necessary to insure good judgment in the government and discipline of the school.

The value and success of all government depend largely upon the character and ability of those in authority, and this is especially true in the government of the school.

For teachers' certificates of qualification, see above under County and City Superintendents.

QUESTIONS.
1. Who compose the Board of Education?
2. Name some of the duties of this board.
3. What is meant by nomination being subject to confirmation by the Senate?
4. What are school funds?
5. What are by-laws?

6. What are claims payable out of State Funds?
7. What important work is done at the meetings of teachers arranged by the State board of Education?
8. What very important duty has the State Board to perform in reference to books?
9. What are the general duties of the board?
10. How is the superintendent of public instruction chosen?
11. What is his salary?
12. What are his duties?
13. What is the public free school system?
14. What is the extent of the power of the superintendent of public instruction?
15. How often does the superintendent report to the General Assembly, and what information does his report contain?
16. Who appoints county and city superintendents, and what is their term of office?
17. Name some of the duties of these officers.
18. Who compose the School Trustee Electoral Board?
19. What are their duties?
20. Who compose the County School Board?
21. Name some of the duties of this board.
22. How are school districts laid out?
23. How are school trustees chosen, and what is their terra of office?
24. Of whom is the District Board of School Trustees composed?
25. Name some of the powers of this board.
26. Of whom is the City Board of Trustees composed?
27. What is the census of children?
28. What is a scholastic year?
29. Tell what State funds, county funds, and district funds are.
30. Who receives and pays out all school funds?
31. What does the tax of one mill on the dollar mean?
32. From what sources besides the tax on property are school funds obtained?
33. What are the qualifications of teachers?

OUTLINE OF COLONIAL AND STATE HISTORY.

1497. John Cabot discovered Labrador, the basis of the English title to Virginia.

1585. Virginia was so named by Queen Elizabeth in honor of her unmarried state.

1606. Charter granted to the London Company.

1607. Settlement at Jamestown.

John Smith, "the Father of the Colony," rescued from death by Pocahontas, the daughter of Powhatan, the King of the Pamunkey Indians.

1608. John Smith President of the Colony.

1609. The London Company receives its second Charter.

1610. "The Starving Time."

1612. Culture of tobacco commenced.

1613. Pocahontas marries John Rolfe.

1617. Death of Pocahontas at Gravesend, England.

1618. "The Great Charter of Virginia" granted by the London Company.

1619. Slaves landed from a Dutch ship.

First Colonial Assembly meets at Jamestown, July 30.

1621. Formal grant of free government by a written charter.

A Council of State and a General Assembly established--the model of every subsequent provincial form of government.

1622. Massacre of settlers by Indians under Opechancanough.

1624. Fall of the London Company.

Virginia becomes a royal province.

1644. Second Indian Massacre. Opechancanough captured and killed.

1652-60. Virginia under the Commonwealth.

1660. Called the "Old Dominion."

Navigation Acts put into operation by British Government.
1673. Grant to Lords Culpeper and Arlington of immense estates by Charles II.
1676. Bacon's Rebellion. 1693. William and Mary College chartered.
Postal System adopted.
1698. The seat of government removed to Williamsburg.
1699. The Huguenots settle in Virginia.
1700. First Commencement of William and Mary College.
1732. Scotch-Irish and Germans settle in the Shenandoah Valley.
George Washington born February 22.
1733. Founding of Richmond at the Falls of the James.
1736. First Virginia Newspaper--"The Virginia Gazette."
Norfolk incorporated.
1737. Richmond laid out by Col. William Byrd.
1742. Richmond incorporated.
1743. Thomas Jefferson born April 2.
1754. The French and Indian War begun. Battle of Great Meadows.
French defeated by Colonists under George Washington.
1755. Braddock defeated in his attack on Fort Duquesne.
1758. Fort Duquesne captured by English and Virginia troops.
1763. "The Parsons' Case." Patrick Henry's Famous Speech.
End of the French and Indian War.
1764. Battle of Point Pleasant (now in West Virginia).
1765. Resolutions of the House of Burgesses against taxation without representation.
1765. The British Parliament passes the Stamp Act.
1766. Stamp Act repealed by Parliament.
1767. Parliament imposes a tax on tea and other articles.
1769. Virginia resolves passed by the House of Burgesses, May 16.
1774. The first Continental Congress met at Philadelphia, September 9.
1775. Convention at Richmond "to organize a provincial form of government and a plan of defense for the Colony."
End of royal government in Virginia. Committee of Safety appointed.
1776. Constitution and Bill of Rights adopted.

Declaration of Independence written by Thomas Jefferson signed in Philadelphia, July 4.

1779. The seat of government removed to Richmond.

Conquest of the Northwest Territory by Col. George Rogers Clarke.

1780. Virginia troops defeat the British at King's Mountain, October 7.

1781. Richmond captured by British under Benedict Arnold, in January.

Cornwallis surrendered at Yorktown, October 19.

Cession of the Northwest Territory to the Federal Government.

1785. Act of Religious Freedom.

1787. Constitution of the United States adopted in convention of which George Washington was President.

1788. Ratifies the Constitution of the United States.

1789. Washington inaugurated first President of the United States, April 30.

1799. George Washington died December 14.

1807. Robert E. Lee born January 19.

1819. University of Virginia established.

1826. Thomas Jefferson died July 1.

1830. Constitution of the State amended.

1852. Constitution of the State again amended.

1859. John Brown's attack on Harper's Ferry.

1861. Ordinance of Secession passed by the Convention.

Richmond the Capital of the Southern Confederacy.

Confederate Congress assembled at Richmond, July 20.

First battle of Manassas, July 21.

1861-65. Virginia the principal battle ground of the "War between the States."

1862. Battle between the "Virginia" and the "Monitor," March 9.

1863. West Virginia formed and admitted to the Union.

1865. Provisional Government established in Virginia, May 9.

1869. Constitution amended.

Virginia readmitted to the Union.

1870. State enacts a liberal system of public education.

Robert E. Lee died October 12.

1881. Centennial of the surrender of Cornwallis at Yorktown.

1902. New Constitution in force July 10.

COLONIAL GOVERNORS.

1607. Capt. Edward Maria Wingfield, President of the Council under first Charter of the London Company.

Capt. John Ratcliffe, President of the Council.

1608. Capt. John Smith, President of the Council.

1609. Sir George Percy, Acting President of the Council.

1610. Lord Delaware, first Governor under new Charter of 1609. Sir Thomas Gates, Lieutenant-Governor under Lord Delaware.

1611. Sir Thomas Dale, High Marshal under Lord Delaware.

1616. Sir George Yeardley, Lieutenant-Governor under Lord Delaware.

1617. Samuel Argall, Lieutenant-Governor under Lord Delaware.

1619. Sir George Yeardley, first Governor under the "Great Charter of Virginia" granted by the London Company.

1621. Sir Francis Wyatt, second Governor under the "Great Charter." Put into effect the new constitution.

1626. Sir George Yeardley, third Governor under the "Great Charter."

1627. Francis West, fourth Governor under the "Great Charter."

1629. John Potts, fifth Governor under the "Great Charter."

Sir John Harvey, first Royal Governor, appointed by King Charles I.

1635. John West, acting Governor, in place of Harvey deposed by the people.

1636. Sir John Harvey, reinstated by the King.

1639. Sir Francis Wyatt, Royal Governor.

1642. Sir William Berkeley, Royal Governor. Deposed by the Commonwealth in 1652.

1652. Richard Bennett, first Governor under the Commonwealth.

1655. Edward Digges, second Governor under the Commonwealth.

1656. Samuel Matthews, third Governor under the Commonwealth.

1660. Sir William Berkeley elected by the House of Burgesses and reappointed by Charles II. after the Restoration.

1661. Col. Francis Moryson, Acting Governor.

1663. Sir William Berkeley reappointed and continued to act as Governor until 1677.

1675. Lord Culpeper appointed Royal Governor for life by Charles II., but did not act as such until 1680.

1677. Sir Herbert Jeffreys, Lieutenant-Governor and Acting Governor in absence of Lord Culpeper.

1678. Sir Henry Chickeley, Lieutenant-Governor and Acting Governor in absence of Lord Culpeper.

1684. Lord Howard of Effingham appointed Governor to succeed Lord Culpeper, deposed in 1683.

1688. Nathaniel Bacon, Lieutenant-Governor and Acting Governor.

1690. Francis Nicholson, first Royal Governor appointed after the Revolution of 1688.

1692. Sir Edmund Andros, Royal Governor. Founded William and Mary College.

1698. Francis Nicholson, Royal Governor. Removed capital to Williamsburg.

1704. George Hamilton Douglas, Earl of Orkney, Royal Governor.

1705. Edward Scott, Lieutenant-Governor and Acting Governor.

1706. Edmund Jennings, Lieutenant-Governor and Acting Governor.

1710. Robert Hunter, Lieutenant-Governor and Acting Governor.

Alexander Spotswood, Lieutenant-Governor and Acting Governor.

1722. Hugh Drysdale, Lieutenant-Governor and Acting Governor.

1726. Robert Carter, Lieutenant-Governor and Acting Governor.

1727. William Gooch, Lieutenant-Governor and Acting Governor.

1737. William A. Keppel, Earl of Albemarle, Royal Governor.

1749. John Robinson, Lieutenant-Governor and Acting Governor.

1750. Thomas Lee, Lieutenant-Governor. Died immediately after his appointment.

Louis Burwell, Lieutenant-Governor and Acting Governor.

1752. Robert Dinwiddie, Lieutenant-Governor. First explored the Valley.

1756. John Campbell, Earl of Loudoun, Royal Governor.

Robert Dinwiddie, Lieutenaut-Governor and Acting Governor.
1758. John Blair, Lieutenant-Governor and Acting Governor.
Francis Fauqmer, Lieutenant-Governor and Acting Governor.
1763. Jeffrey Amherst, Lord Amherst, Royal Governor.
1768. John Blair, Lieutenant-Governor and Acting Governor.
Norborne Berkeley, Lord Botetourt, Royal Governor.
1770. William Nelson, Lieutenant-Governor and Acting Governor.
1772. Lord Dunmore, Royal Governor until the Revolution.
1775. Edmund Pendleton, President of the Committee of Safety.

STATE GOVERNORS.

1776-1779. Patrick Henry.
1779-1781. Thomas Jefferson.
1781.   Thomas Nelson.
1781-1784. Benjamin Harrison.
1784-1786. Patrick Henry.
1786-1788. Edmund Randolph.
1788-1791. Beverly Randolph.
1791-1794. Henry Lee.
1794-1796. Robert Brooks.
1796-1799. James Wood.
1799-1802. James Monroe.
1802-1805. John Page
1805-1808. William H. Cabell.
1808-1811. John Tyler.
1811.   James Monroe.
1811-1812. George William Smith, Lieutenant-Governor.
1812-1814. James Barbour.
1814-1816. Wilson Cary Nichols.
1816-1819. James P. Preston.

1819-1822. Thomas M. Randolph.
1822-1825. James Pleasants.
1825-1827. John Tyler.
1827-1830. William B. Giles.
1830-1834. John Floyd.
1834-1836. Littleton Waller Tazewell.
1836-1837. Wyndham Robertson, Lieutenant-Governor.
1837-1840. David Campbell.
1840-1841. Thomas Walker Gilmer.
1841.　　　John M. Patton.
1841-1842. John Rutherford. Lieutenant-Governor.
1842-1843. John M. Gregory.
1843-1846. James McDowell.
1846-1849. William Smith.
1849-1852. John B. Floyd.
1852-1856. Joseph Johnson.
1856-1860. Henry Alexander Wise.
1860-1864. John Letcher.
1864-1865. William Smith.
1865-1868. Francis H. Pierpont.
1868-1869. Henry H. Wells.
1869-1873. Gilbert C. Walker.
1873-1877. James L. Kempner.
1877-1881. Frederick W. M. Holliday.
1881-1885. William E. Gameron.
1885-1889. Fitzhugh Lee.
1889-1893. Philip W. McKinney.
1893-1897. Charles T. O'Ferrall.
1897.　　　J. Hoge Tyler.
1901.　　　A. J. Montague.

CONSTITUTION OF VIRGINIA.

Whereas, pursuant to an act of the General Assembly of Virginia, approved March the fifth, in the year of our Lord nineteen hundred, the question, "shall there be a convention to revise the Constitution and amend the same?" was submitted to the electors of the State of Virginia, qualified to vote for members of the General Assembly, at an election held throughout the State on the fourth Thursday in May, in the year nineteen hundred, at--which election a majority of the electors so qualified voting at said election did decide in favor of a convention for such purpose; and,

Whereas, the General Assembly at its next session did provide by law for the election of delegates to such convention, in pursuance whereof the members of this Convention were elected by the good people of Virginia, to meet in convention for such purpose.

We, therefore, the people of Virginia, so assembled in Convention through our representatives, with gratitude to God for His past favors, and invoking His blessings upon the result of our deliberations, do ordain and establish the following revised and amended Constitution for the government of the Commonwealth:

ARTICLE I.
BILL OF RIGHTS.

A DECLARATION OF RIGHTS, made by the representatives of the good people of Virginia assembled in full and free Convention; which rights do pertain to them and their posterity, as the Basis mid Foundation of Government.

SECTION 1. That all men are by nature equally free and independent, and have certain inherent rights, of which, when they enter into a state of society, they cannot, by any compact, deprive or divest their posterity, namely, the enjoyment of life and liberty, with the means of acquiring and possessing property, and pursuing and obtaining happiness and safety.

SEC. 2. That all power is vested in, and consequently derived from, the people; that magistrates are their trustees and servants, and at all times amenable to them.

SEC. 3. That government is, or ought to be, instituted for the common benefit, protection and security of the people, nation or community; of all the various modes and forms of government, that is best, which is capable of producing the greatest degree of happiness and safety, and is most effectually secured against the danger of maladministration; and, whenever any government shall be found inadequate or contrary to these purposes, a majority of the community hath an indubitable, inalienable, and indefeasible right to reform, alter or abolish it, in such manner as shall be judged most conducive to the public weal.

SEC. 4. That no man, or set of men, is entitled to exclusive or separate emoluments or privileges from the community, but in consideration of public services, which not being descendible, neither ought the offices of magistrate, legislator or judge to be hereditary.

SEC 5 That the legislative executive, and judicial departments of the State should be separate and distinct, and that the members thereof may be restrained from oppression, by feeling and participating the burthens of the people, they should, at fixed periods, be reduced to a private station, return into that body from which they were originally taken, and the vacancies be supplied by regular elections, in which all or any part of the former members shall be again eligible, or ineligible, as the laws may direct

SEC 6 That all elections should be free, and that all men, having sufficient evidence of permanent common interest with, and attachment to, the community, have the right of suffrage, and can not be taxed, or deprived of, or damaged in, their property for public uses without their own consent, or that of their representatives duly elected, or bound by any law to which they have not, in like manner, assented for the public good

SEC 7 That all power of suspending laws, or the execution of laws, by any authority, without consent of the representatives of the people, is injurious to their rights, and ought not to be exercised

SEC 8 That no man shall be deprived of his life, or liberty, except by the law of the land, or the judgment of his peers, nor shall any man be compelled in any criminal proceeding to give evidence against himself, nor be put twice in jeopardy for the same offence, but an appeal may be allowed to the Commonwealth in all prosecutions for the violation of a law relating to the state revenue

That in all criminal prosecutions a man hath a right to demand the cause and nature of his accusation, to be confronted with the accusers and witnesses, to call for evidence in his favor, and to a speedy trial by an impartial jury of his vicinage, without whose unanimous consent he cannot be found guilty, provided, however, that in any criminal case, upon a plea of guilty, tendered in person by the accused, and with the consent of the attorney for the Commonwealth, entered of record, the court shall, and in a prosecution for an offence not punishable by death, or confinement in the penitentiary, upon a plea of not guilty, with the consent of the accused, given in person and of the attorney for the Commonwealth, both entered of record, the court, in its discretion, may hear and determine the case, without the intervention of a jury, and, that the General Assembly may provide for the trial of offences not punishable by death, or confinement in the penitentiary, by a justice of the peace, without a jury, preserving in all such cases, the right of the accused to an appeal to and trial by jury in the circuit or corporation court, and may also provide for juries consisting of less than twelve, but not less than five, for the trial of offences not punishable by death, or confinement in the penitentiary, and may classify such cases, and prescribe the number of jurors for each class

SEC 9 That excessive bail ought not to be required, nor excessive fines imposed, nor cruel and unusual punishments inflicted

SEC 10 That general warrants, whereby an officer or messenger may be commanded to search suspected places without evidence of a fact committed, or to seize any person or persons not named or whose offence is not particularly described and supported by evidence, are grievous and oppressive, and ought not to be granted

SEC 11 That no person shall be deprived of his property without due process of law, and in controversies respecting property, and in suits between man and man, trial by jury is preferable to any other and ought to be held sacred, but the General Assembly may limit the number of jurors for civil cases in circuit and corporation courts to not less than five in cases now cognizable by justices of the peace, or to not less than seven in cases not so cognizable

SEC 12 That the freedom of the press is one of the great bulwarks of liberty, and can never be restrained but by despotic governments, and any citizen may freely speak, write and publish his sentiments on all subjects, being responsible for the abuse of that right

SEC 13 That a well regulated milita, composed of the body of the people, trained to arms, is the proper, natural and safe defence of a free state, that standing armies, in time of peace, should be avoided as dangerous to liberty, and that in all cases the military should be under strict subordination to, and governed by, the civil power

SEC 14 That the people have a right to uniform government, and, therefore, that no government separate from, or independent of, the government of Virginia, ought to be erected or established within the limits therof

SEC 15 That no free government, or the blessing of liberty, can be preserved to any people, but by a firm adherence to justice, moderation, temperance, frugality and virtue, and by frequent recurrence to fundamental principles

SEC 16 That religion, or the duty which we owe to our Creator, and the manner of discharging it, can be directed only by reason and conviction, not by force or violence, and, therefore, all men are equally entitled to the free exercise of religion, according to the dictates of conscience, and that it is the mutual duty of all to practice Christian forbearance, love and charity towards each other

SEC 17 The rights enumerated in this Bill of Rights shall not be construed to limit other rights of the people not therein expressed.

ARTICLE II
ELECTIVE FRANCHISE AND QUALIFICATIONS FOR OFFICE

SEC 18 Every male citizen of the United States, twenty one years of age, who has been a resident of the State two years, of the county, city, or town one year, and of the precinct in which he offers to vote, thirty days, next preceding the election in which he offers to vote, has been registered, and has paid his state poll taxes, as hereinafter required, shall be entitled to vote for members of the General Assembly and all officers elective by the people; but removal from one precinct to another, in the same county, city or town shall not deprive any person of his right to vote in the precinct from which he has moved, until the expiration of thirty days after such removal.

SEC. 19. There shall be general registrations in the counties, cities and towns of the State during the years nineteen hundred and two and nineteen hundred and three at such times and in such manner as may be prescribed by an ordinance of this Convention. At such registrations every male citizen of the United States having the qualifications of age and residence required in section Eighteen shall be entitled to register, if he be:

First. A person who, prior to the adoption of this Constitution, served in time of war in the army or navy of the United States, of the Confederate States, or of any state of the United States or of the Confederate States; or,

Second. A son of any such person; or,

Third. A person, who owns property, upon which, for the year next preceding that in which he offers to register, state taxes aggregating at least one dollar have been paid; or,

Fourth. A person able to read any section of this Constitution submitted to him by the officers of registration and to give a reasonable explanation of the same; or, if unable to read such section, able to understand and give a reasonable explanation thereof when read to him by the officers.

A roll containing the names of all persons thus registered, sworn to and certified by the officers of registration, shall be filed, for record and preservation, in the clerk's office of the circuit court of the county, or the clerk's office of the corporation court of the city, as the case may be. Persons thus enrolled shall not be required to register again, unless they shall have ceased to be residents of the State, or become disqualified by section Twenty-three. Any person denied registration under this section shall have the right of appeal to the circuit court of his county, or the corporation court of his city, or to the judge thereof in vacation.

SEC. 20. After the first day of January, nineteen hundred and four, every male citizen of the United States, having the qualifications of age and residence required in section Eighteen, shall be entitled to register, provided:

First. That he has personally paid to the proper officer all state poll taxes assessed or assessable against him, under this or the former Constitution, for the three years next preceding that in which he offers to register; or, if he come of age at such time that no poll tax shall have been assessable against him for the year preceding the year in which he offers to register, has paid one dollar and fifty cents, in satisfaction of the first year's poll tax assessable against him; and,

Second. That, unless physically unable, he make application to register in his own handwriting, without aid, suggestion, or memorandum, in the presence of the registration officers, stating therein his name, age, date and place of birth, residence and occupation at the time and for the two years next preceding, and whether he has previously voted, and, if so, the state, county, and precinct in which he voted last; and,

Third. That he answer on oath any and all questions affecting his qualifications as an elector, submitted to him by the officers of registration, which questions, and his answers thereto, shall be reduced to writing, certified by the said officers, and preserved as a part of their official records.

SEC. 21. Any person registered under either of the last two sections, shall have the right to vote for members of the General Assembly and all officers elective by the people, subject to the following conditions:

That he, unless exempted by section Twenty-two, shall, as a prerequisite to the right to vote after the first day of January, nineteen hundred and four, personally pay, at least six months prior to the election, all state poll taxes assessed or assessable against him, under this Constitution, during the three years next preceding that in which he offers to vote; provided that, if he register after the first day of January, nineteen hundred and four, he shall, unless physically unable, prepare and deposit his ballot without aid, on such printed form as the law may prescribe; but any voter registered prior to that date may be aided in the preparation of his ballot by such officer of election as he himself may designate.

SEC. 22. No person who, during the late war between the States, served in the army or navy of the United States, or the Confederate States, or any state of the United States, or of the Confederate States, shall at any time be required to pay a poll tax as a prerequisite to the right to register or vote. The collection of the state poll tax assessed against any one shall not be enforced by legal process until the same has become three years past due.

SEC. 23. The following persons shall be excluded from registering and voting: Idiots, insane persons, and paupers; persons who, prior to the adoption of this Constitution, were disqualified from voting, by conviction of crime, either within or without this State, and whose disabilities shall not have been removed; persons convicted after the adoption of this Constitution, either within or without this State, of treason, or of any felony, bribery, petit larceny, obtaining money or property under false pretences, embezzlement, forgery, or perjury; persons who, while citizens of this State, after the adoption of this Constitution, have fought a duel with a deadly weapon, or sent or accepted a challenge to fight such duel, either within or without this State, or knowingly conveyed a challenge, or aided or assisted in any way in the fighting of such duel.

SEC. 24. No officer, soldier, seaman, or marine of the United States army or navy shall be deemed to have gained a residence as to the right of suffrage, in the State, or in any county, city or town thereof, by reason of being stationed therein; nor shall an inmate of any charitable institution or a student in any institution of learning, be regarded as having either gained or lost a residence, as to the right of suffrage, by reason of his location or sojourn in such institution.

SEC. 25. The General Assembly shall provide for the annual registration of voters under section Twenty, for an appeal by any person denied registration, for the correction of illegal or fraudulent registration, thereunder, and also for the proper transfer of all voters registered under this Constitution.

SEC. 26. Any person who, in respect to age or residence, would be qualified to vote at the next election, shall be admitted to registration, notwithstanding that at the time thereof he is not so qualified, and shall be entitled to vote at said election if then qualified under the provisions of this Constitution.

SEC. 27. All elections by the people shall be by ballot; all elections by any representative body shall be viva voce, and the vote recorded in the journal thereof.

The ballot-box shall be kept in public view during all elections, and shall not be opened, nor the ballots canvassed or counted, in secret.

So far as consistent with the provisions of this Constitution, the absolute secrecy of the ballot shall be maintained.

SEC. 28. The General Assembly shall provide for ballots without any distinguishing mark or symbol, for use in all state, county, city, and other elections by the people, and the form thereof shall be the same in all places where any such election is held. All ballots shall contain the names of the candidates, and of the offices to be filled, in, clear print and in due and orderly succession; but any voter may erase any name and insert another.

SEC. 29. No voter, during the time of holding any election at which he is entitled to vote, shall be compelled to perform military service, except in time of war or public danger; to attend any court as suitor, juror, or witness; and no voter shall be subject to arrest under any civil process during his attendance at election or in going to or returning therefrom.

SEC. 30. The General Assembly may prescribe a property qualification not exceeding two hundred and fifty dollars for voters in any county or subdivision thereof, or city or town, as a prerequisite for voting in any election for officers, other than the members of the General Assembly, to be wholly elected by the voters of such county or subdivision thereof, or city, or town; such action, if taken, to be had upon the initiative of a representative in the General Assembly of the county, city, or town affected: provided, that the General Assembly in its discretion may make such exemptions from the operation of said property qualification as shall not be in conflict with the Constitution of the United States.

SEC. 31. There shall be in each county and city an electoral board, composed of three members, appointed by the circuit court of the county-court--the corporation court of the city, or the judge of the court in vacation. Of those first appointed, one shall be appointed for a term of one year, one for a term of two years, and one for a term of three years; and thereafter their successors shall be appointed for the full term of three years. Any vacancy occurring in any board shall be filled by the same authority for the unexpired term.

Each electoral board shall appoint the judges, clerks, and registrars of election for its county or city; and, in appointing judges of election, representation as far as possible shall be given to each of the two political parties which, at the general election next preceding their appointment, cast the highest and next highest number of votes. No person, nor the deputy of any person, holding any office or post of profit or emolument, under the United States Government, or who is in the employment of such government, or holding any elective office of profit or trust in the State, or in any county, city, or town thereof, shall be appointed a member of the electoral board, or registrar, or judge of election.

SEC. 32. Every person qualified to vote shall be eligible to any office of the State or of any county, city, town, or other subdivision of the State, wherein he resides, except as otherwise provided in this Constitution, and except that this provision as to residence shall not apply to any office elective by the people where the law provides otherwise. Men and women eighteen years of age shall be eligible to the office of notary public, and qualified to execute the bonds required of them in that capacity.

SEC. 33. The terms of all officers elected under this Constitution shall begin on the first day of February next succeeding their election, unless otherwise provided in this Constitution. All officers, elected or appointed, shall continue to discharge the duties of their offices after their terms of service have expired until their successors have qualified.

SEC. 34. Members of the General Assembly and all officers, executive and judicial, elected or appointed after this Constitution goes into effect, shall, before they enter on the performance of their public duties, severally take and subscribe the following oath or affirmation:

"I do solemnly swear (or affirm) that I will support the Constitution of the United States, and the Constitution of the State of Virginia ordained by the Convention which assembled in the city of Richmond on the twelfth day of June, nineteen hundred and one, and that I will faithfully and impartially discharge and perform all the duties incumbent on me as, according to the best of my ability; so help me God."

SEC. 35. No person shall vote at any legalized primary election for the nomination of any candidate for office unless he is at the time registered and qualified to vote at the next succeeding election.

SEC. 36. The General Assembly shall enact such laws as are necessary and proper for the purpose of securing the regularity and purity of general, local and primary elections, and preventing and punishing any corrupt practices in connection therewith; and shall have power, in addition to other penalties and punishments now or hereafter prescribed by law for such offences, to provide that persons convicted of them shall thereafter be disqualified from voting or holding office.

SEC. 37. The General Assembly may provide for the use, throughout the State or in any one or more counties, cities, or towns in any election, of machines for receiving, recording, and counting the votes cast thereat: provided, that the secrecy of the voting be not thereby impaired.

SEC. 38. After the first day of January, nineteen hundred and four, the treasurer of each county and city shall, at least five months before each regular election, file with the clerk of the circuit court of his county, or of the corporation court of his city, a list of all persons in his county or city, who have paid not later than six months prior to such election, the state poll taxes required by this Constitution during the three years next preceding that in which such election is held; which list shall be arranged alphabetically, by magisterial districts or wards, shall state the white and colored persons separately, and shall be verified by the oath of the treasurer. The clerk, within ten days from the receipt of the list, shall make and certify a sufficient number of copies thereof, and shall deliver one copy for each voting place in his county or city, to the sheriff of the county or sergeant of the city, whose duty it shall be to post one copy, without delay, at each of the voting places, and, within ten days from the receipt thereof, to make return on oath to the clerk, as to the places where and dates at which said copies were respectively posted; which return the clerk shall record in a book kept in his office for the purpose; and he shall keep in his office for public inspection, for at least sixty days after receiving the list, not less than ten certified copies thereof, and also cause the list to be published in such other manner as may be prescribed by law; the original list returned by the treasurer shall be filed and preserved by the clerk among the public records of his office for at least five years after receiving the same. Within thirty days after the list has been so posted, any person who shall have paid his capitation tax, but whose name is omitted from the certified list, may, after five days' written notice to the treasurer, apply to the circuit court of his county, or corporation court of his city, or to the judge thereof in vacation, to have the same corrected and his name entered thereon, which application the court or judge shall promptly hear and decide.

The clerk shall deliver, or cause to be delivered, with the poll-books, at a reasonable time before every election, to one of the judges of election of each precinct of his county or city, a like certified copy of the list, which shall be conclusive evidence of the facts therein stated for the purpose of voting. The clerk shall also,--within sixty days after the filing of the list by the treasurer, forward a certified copy thereof, with such corrections as may have been made by order of the court or judge, to the Auditor of Public Accounts, who shall charge the amount of the poll taxes stated therein to such treasurer unless previously accounted for.

Further evidence of the prepayment of the capitation taxes required by this Constitution, as a prerequisite to the right to register and vote, may be prescribed by law.

ARTICLE III.
DIVISION OF POWERS.

SEC. 39. Except as hereinafter provided, the legislative, executive, and judiciary departments shall be separate and distinct, so that neither exercise the powers properly belonging to either of the others, nor any person exercise the power of more than one of them at the same time.

ARTICLE IV.
LEGISLATIVE DEPARTMENT.

SEC. 40. The legislative power of the State shall be vested in a General Assembly, which shall consist of a Senate and House of Delegates.

SEC. 41. The Senate shall consist of not more than forty and not less than thirty-three members, who shall be elected quadrennially by the voters of the several senatorial districts, on the Tuesday succeeding the first Monday in November.

SEC. 42. The House of Delegates shall consist of not more than one hundred and not less than ninety members, who shall be elected biennially by the voters of the several house districts, on the Tuesday succeeding the first Monday in November.

SEC. 43. The apportionment of the State into senatorial and house districts, made by the acts of the General Assembly, approved April the second, nineteen hundred and two, is hereby adopted; but a re-apportionment may be made in the year nineteen hundred and six, and shall be made in the year nineteen hundred and twelve, and every tenth year thereafter.

SEC. 44. Any person may be elected senator who, at the time of election, is actually a resident of the senatorial district and qualified to vote for members of the General Assembly; and any person may be elected a member of the House of Delegates who, at the time of election, is actually a resident of the house district and qualified to vote for members of the General Assembly. But no person holding a salaried office under the state government, and no judge of any court, attorney for the Commonwealth, sheriff, sergeant, treasurer, assessor of taxes, commissioner of the revenue, collector of taxes, or clerk of any court, shall be a member of either house of the General Assembly during his continuance in office, and the election of any such person to either house of the General Assembly, and his qualification as a member thereof, shall vacate any such office held by him; and no person holding any office or post of profit or emolument under the United States Government or who is in the employment of such government, shall be eligible to either house. The removal of a senator or delegate from the district for which he is elected, shall vacate his office.

SEC. 45. The members of the General Assembly shall receive for their services a salary to be fixed by law and paid from the public treasury; but no act increasing such salary shall take effect until after the end of the term for which the members voting thereon were elected; and no member during the term for which he shall have been elected, shall be appointed or elected to any civil office of profit in the State except offices filled by election by the people.

SEC. 46. The General Assembly shall meet once in two years on the second Wednesday in January next succeeding the election of the members of the House of Delegates and not oftener unless convened in the manner prescribed by this Constitution. No session of the General Assembly, after the first under this Constitution, shall continue longer than sixty days; but with the concurrence of three-fifths of the members elected to each house, the session may be extended for a period not exceeding thirty days. Except for the first session held under this Constitution, members shall be allowed a salary for not exceeding sixty days at any regular session, and for not exceeding thirty days at any extra session. Neither house shall, without the consent of the other, adjourn to another place nor for more than three days. A majority of the members elected to each house shall constitute a quorum to do business, but a smaller number may adjourn from day to day, and shall have power to compel the attendance of members in such manner and under such penalty as each house may prescribe.

SEC. 47. The House of Delegates shall choose its own speaker; and, in the absence of the Lieutenant-Governor, or when he shall exercise the office of Governor, the Senate shall choose from their own body a president pro tempore. Each house shall select its officers, settle its rules of procedure, and direct writs of election for supplying vacancies which may occur during the session of the General Assembly; but, if vacancies occur during the recess, such writs may be issued by the Governor, under such regulations as may be prescribed by law. Each house shall judge of the election, qualification, and returns of its members; may punish them for disorderly behavior, and, with the concurrence of two-thirds, expel a member.

SEC. 48. Members of the General Assembly shall, in all cases, except treason, felony, or breach of the peace, be privileged from arrest during the sessions of their respective houses; and for any speech or debate in either house shall not be questioned in any other place. They shall not be subject to arrest, under any civil process, during the sessions of the General Assembly, or the fifteen days next before the beginning or after the ending of any session.

SEC. 49. Each house shall keep a journal of its proceedings, which shall be published from time to time, and the yeas and nays of the members of either house on any question shall, at the desire of one-fifth of those present, be entered on the journal.

SEC. 50. No law shall be enacted except by bill. A bill may originate in either house, to be approved or rejected by the other, or may be amended by either, with the concurrence of the other.

No bill shall become a law unless, prior to its passage, it has been,

(a) Referred to a committee of each house, considered by such committee in session, and reported;

(b) Printed by the house, in which it originated, prior to its passage therein;

(c) Read at length on three different calendar days in each house; and unless,

(d) A yea and nay vote has been taken in each house upon its final passage, the names of the members voting for and against entered on the journal, and a majority of those voting, which shall include at least two-fifths of the members elected to each house, recorded in the affirmative.

And only in the manner required in subdivision (d) of this section shall an amendment to a bill by one house be concurred in by the other, or a conference report be adopted by either house, or either house discharge a committee from the consideration of a bill and consider the same as if reported; provided that the printing and reading, or either, required in subdivisions (b) and (c) of this section, may be dispensed with in a bill to codify the laws of the State, and in any case of emergency by a vote of four- fifths of the members voting in each house taken by the yeas and nays, the names of the members voting for and against, entered on the journal; and provided further, that no bill which creates, or establishes a new office, or which creates, continues, or revives a debt or charge, or makes, continues or revives any appropriation of public or trust money, or property, or releases, discharges or commutes any claim or demand of the State, or which imposes, continues or revives a tax, shall be passed except by the affirmative vote of a majority of all the members elected to each house, the vote to be by the yeas and nays, and the names of the members voting for and against, entered on the journal. Every law imposing, continuing or reviving a tax shall specifically state such tax and no law shall be construed as so stating such tax, which requires a reference to any other law or any other tax. The presiding officer of each house shall, in the presence of the house over which he presides, sign every bill that has been passed by both houses and duly enrolled. Immediately before this is done, all other business being suspended, the title of the bill shall be publicly read. The fact of signing shall be entered on the journal.

SEC. 51. There shall be a joint committee of the General Assembly, consisting of seven members appointed by the House of Delegates, and five members appointed by the Senate, which shall be a standing committee on special, private, and local legislation. Before reference to a committee, as provided by section Fifty, any special, private, or local bill introduced in either house shall be referred to and considered by such joint committee and returned to the house in which it originated with a statement in writing whether the object of the bill can be accomplished under general law or by court proceeding; whereupon, the bill, with the accompanying statement, shall take the course provided by section Fifty. The joint committee may be discharged from the consideration of a bill by the house in which it originated in the manner provided in section Fifty for the discharge of other committees.

SEC. 52. No law shall embrace more than one object, which shall be expressed in its title; nor shall any law be revived or amended with reference to its title, but the act revived or the section amended shall be re-enacted and published at length.

SEC. 53. No law, except a general appropriation law, shall take effect until at least ninety days after the adjournment of the session of the General Assembly at which it is enacted, unless in case of an emergency (which emergency shall be expressed in the body of the bill), the General Assembly shall otherwise direct by a vote of four-fifths of the members voting in each house, such vote to be taken by the yeas and nays, and the names of the members voting for and against entered on the journal.

SEC. 54. The Governor, Lieutenant-Governor, Attorney-General, judges, members of the State Corporation Commission, and executive officers at the seat of government, and all officers appointed by the Governor or elected by the General Assembly, offending against the State by malfeasance in office, corruption, neglect of duty, or other high crime or misdemeanor, may be impeached by the House of Delegates, and prosecuted before the Senate which shall have the sole power to try impeachment. When sitting for that purpose, the senators shall be on oath or affirmation, and no person shall be convicted without the concurrence of two-thirds of the senators present. Judgment in case of impeachment shall not extend further than removal from office and disqualification to hold and enjoy any office of honor, trust, or profit under the State; but the person convicted shall nevertheless be subject to indictment, trial, judgment, and punishment according to law. The Senate may sit during the recess of the General Assembly for the trial of impeachments.

SEC. 55. The General Assembly shall by law apportion the State into districts, corresponding with the number of representatives to which it may be entitled in the House of Representatives of the Congress of the United States; which districts shall be composed of contiguous and compact territory containing, as nearly as practicable, an equal number of inhabitants.

SEC. 56. The manner of conducting and making returns of elections, of determining contested elections, and of filling vacancies in office, in cases not specially provided for by this Constitution, shall be prescribed by law, and the General Assembly may declare the cases in which any office shall be deemed vacant where no provision is made for that purpose in this Constitution.

SEC. 57. The General Assembly shall have power, by a two-thirds vote, to remove disabilities incurred under section Twenty-three, of Article Two, of this Constitution, with reference to duelling.

SEC. 58. The privilege of the writ of habeas corpus shall not be suspended unless when in cases of invasion or rebellion, the public safety may require. The General Assembly shall not pass any bill of attainder, or any ex post facto law, or any law impairing the obligation of contracts, or any law abridging the freedom of speech or of the press. It shall not enact any law whereby private property shall be taken or damaged for public uses, without just compensation. No man shall be compelled to frequent or support any religious worship, place, or ministry whatsoever, nor shall be enforced, restrained, molested, or burthened in his body or goods, nor shall otherwise suffer on account of his religious opinions or belief; but all men shall be free to profess, and by argument to maintain, their opinions in matters of religion, and the same shall in no wise diminish, enlarge, or affect their civil capacities. And the General Assembly shall not prescribe any religious test whatever, or confer any peculiar privileges or advantages on any sect or denomination, or pass any law requiring or authorizing any religious society, or the people of any district within this State, to levy on themselves or others any tax for the erection or repair of any house of public worship, or for the support of any church or ministry; but it shall be left free to every person to select his religious instructor, and to make for his support such private contract as he shall please.

SEC. 59. The General Assembly shall not grant a charter of incorporation to any church or religious denomination, but may secure the title to church property to an extent to be limited by law.

SEC. 60. No lottery shall hereafter be authorized by law; and the buying, selling, or transferring of tickets or chances in any lottery shall be prohibited.

SEC. 61. No new county shall be formed with an area of less than six hundred square miles; nor shall the county or counties from which it is formed be reduced below that area; nor shall any county be reduced in population below eight thousand. But any county, the length of which is three times its mean breadth, or which exceeds fifty miles in length, may be divided at the discretion of the General Assembly.

SEC. 62. The General Assembly shall have full power to enact local option or dispensary laws, or any other laws controlling, regulating, or prohibiting the manufacture or sale of intoxicating liquors.

SEC. 63. The General Assembly shall confer on the courts power to grant divorces, change the names of persons, and direct the sale of estates belonging to infants and other persons under legal disabilities, and shall not, by special legislation, grant relief in these or other cases of which the courts or other tribunals may have jurisdiction. The General Assembly may regulate the exercise by courts of the right to punish for contempt. The General Assembly shall not enact any local, special, or private law in the following cases:--

1. For the punishment of crime.

2. Providing a change of venue in civil or criminal cases.

3. Regulating the practice in, or the jurisdiction of, or changing the rules of evidence in any judicial proceedings or inquiry before, the courts or other tribunals, or providing or changing the methods of collecting debts or enforcing judgments, or prescribing the effect of judicial sales of real estate.

4. Changing or locating county seats.

5. For the assessment and collection of taxes, except as to animals which the General Assembly may deem dangerous to the farming interests.

6. Extending the time for the assessment or collection of taxes.

7. Exempting property from taxation.

8. Remitting, releasing, postponing, or diminishing any obligation or liability of any person, corporation, or association, to the State or to any political subdivision thereof.

9. Refunding money lawfully paid into the treasury of the State or the treasury of any political subdivision thereof.

10. Granting from the treasury of the State, or granting or authorizing to be granted from the treasury of any political subdivision thereof, any extra compensation to any public officer, servant, agent, or contractor.

11. For conducting elections or designating the places of voting.

12. Regulating labor, trade, mining or manufacturing, or the rate of interest on money.

13. Granting any pension or pensions.

14. Creating, increasing, or decreasing, or authorizing to be created, increased, or decreased, the salaries, fees, percentages, or allowances of public officers during the term for which they are elected or appointed.

15. Declaring streams navigable, or authorizing the construction of booms or dams therein, or the removal of obstructions therefrom.

16. Affecting or regulating fencing or the boundaries of land, or the running at large of stock.

17. Creating private corporations, or amending, renewing or extending the charters thereof.

18. Granting to any private corporation, association, or individual any special

or exclusive right, privilege or immunity.

19. Naming or changing the name of any private corporation or association.

20. Remitting the forfeiture of the charter of any private corporation except upon the condition that such corporation shall thereafter hold its charter subject to the provisions of this Constitution and the laws passed in pursuance thereof.

SEC. 64. In all the cases enumerated in the last section, and in every other case which, in its judgment, may be provided for by general laws, the General Assembly shall enact general laws. Any general law shall be subject to amendment or repeal, but the amendment or partial repeal thereof shall not operate directly or indirectly to enact, and shall not have the effect of the enactment of a special, private, or local law.

No general or special law shall surrender or suspend the right and power of the State, or any political subdivision thereof, to tax corporations or corporate property, except as authorized by Article Thirteen. No private corporation, association, or individual shall be specially exempted from the operation of any general law, nor shall its operation be suspended for the benefit of any private corporation, association, or individual.

SEC. 65, The General Assembly may by general laws, confer upon the boards of supervisors of counties, and the councils of cities and towns, such powers of local and special legislation, as it may from time to time deem expedient, not inconsistent with the limitations contained in this Constitution.

SEC. 66. The Clerk of the House of Delegates shall be Keeper of the Rolls of the State but shall receive no compensation from the State for his services as such.

The General Assembly by general law shall prescribe the number of employees of the Senate and House of Delegates, including the clerks thereof, and fix their compensation at a per diem for the time actually employed in the discharge of their duties.

SEC. 67. The General Assembly shall not make any appropriation of public funds, of personal property, or of any real estate, to any church, or sectarian society, association, or institution of any kind whatever, which is entirely or partly, directly or indirectly, controlled by any church or sectarian society; nor shall the General Assembly make any like appropriation to any charitable institution, which is not owned or controlled by the State; except that it may, in its discretion, make appropriations to non-sectarian institutions for the reform of youthful criminals; but nothing herein contained shall prohibit the General Assembly from authorizing counties, cities, or towns to make such appropriations to any charitable institution or association.

SEC. 68. The General Assembly shall, at each regular session, appoint a standing committee, consisting of two members of the Senate and three members of the House of Delegates, which shall be known as the Auditing Committee. Such committee shall annually, or oftener in its discretion, examine the books and accounts of the First Auditor, the State Treasurer, the Secretary of the Commonwealth, and other executive officers at the seat of government whose duties pertain to auditing or accounting for the state revenue, report the result of its investigations to the Governor, and cause the same to be published in two newspapers of general circulation in the State. The Governor shall, at the beginning of each session, submit said reports to the General Assembly for appropriate action. The committee may sit during the recess of the General Assembly, receive such compensation as may be prescribed by law, and employ one or more accountants to assist in its investigations.

ARTICLE V.
EXECUTIVE DEPARTMENT.

SEC. 69. The chief executive power of the State shall be vested in a Governor. He shall hold office for a term of four years, to commence on the first day of February next succeeding his election, and be ineligible to the same office for the term next succeeding that for which he was elected, and to any other office during his term of service.

SEC. 70. The Governor shall be elected by the qualified voters of the State at the time and place of choosing members of the General Assembly. Returns of the election shall be transmitted, under seal, by the proper officers, to the Secretary of the Commonwealth, who shall deliver them to the Speaker of the House of Delegates on the first day of the next session of the General Assembly. The Speaker of the House of Delegates shall, within one week thereafter, in the presence of a majority of the Senate and of the House of Delegates, open the returns, and the votes shall then be counted. The person having the highest number of votes shall be declared elected; but if two or more shall have the highest and an equal number of votes, one of them shall lie chosen Governor by the joint vote of the two houses of the General Assembly. Contested elections for Governor shall be decided by a like vote, and the mode of proceeding in such cases shall be prescribed by law.

SEC. 71. No person except a citizen of the United States shall be eligible to the office of Governor; and if such person be of foreign birth, he must have been a citizen of the United States for ten years next preceding his election; nor shall any person be eligible to that office unless he shall have attained the age of thirty years, and have been a resident of the State for five years next preceding his election.

SEC. 72. The Governor shall reside at the seat of government; shall receive five thousand dollars for each year of his service, and while in office shall receive no other emolument from this or any other government.

SEC. 73. The Governor shall take care that the laws be faithfully executed; communicate to the General Assembly, at every session, the condition of the State; recommend to its consideration such measures as he may deem expedient, and convene the General Assembly on application of two-thirds of the members of both houses thereof, or when, in his opinion, the interest of the State may require. He shall be commander-in-chief of the land and naval forces of the State; have power to embody the militia to repel invasion, suppress insurrection and enforce the execution of the laws; conduct, either in person or in such manner as shall be prescribed by law, all intercourse with other and foreign states; and, during the recess of the General Assembly, shall have power to suspend from office for misbehavior, incapacity, neglect of official duty, or acts performed without due authority of law, all executive officers at the seat of government except the Lieutenant-Governor; but, in any case in which this power is so exercised, the Governor shall report to the General Assembly, at the beginning of the next session thereof, the fact of such suspension and the cause therefor, whereupon the General Assembly shall determine whether such officer shall be restored or finally removed; and the Governor shall have power, during the recess of the General Assembly, to appoint, pro tempore, successors to all officers so suspended, and to fill, pro tempore, vacancies in all offices of the State for the filling of which the Constitution and laws make no other provision; but his appointments to such vacancies shall be by commissions to expire at the end of thirty days after the commencement of the next session of the General Assembly. He shall have power to remit fines and penalties in such cases, and under such rules and regulations, as may be prescribed by law, and except when the prosecution has been carried on by the House of Delegates, to grant reprieves and pardons after conviction; to remove political disabilities consequent upon conviction for offences committed prior or subsequent to the adoption of this Constitution, and to commute capital punishment; but he shall communicate to the General Assembly, at each session, particulars of every case of fine or penalty remitted, of reprieve or pardon granted, and of punishment commuted, with his reasons for remitting, granting, or commuting the same.

SEC. 74. The Governor may require information in writing, under oath, from the officers of the executive department and superintendents of state institutions upon any subject relating to the duties of their respective offices and institutions; and he may inspect at any time their official books, accounts and vouchers, and ascertain the condition of the public funds in their charge, and in that connection may employ accountants. He may require the opinion in writing of the Attorney-General upon any question of law affecting the official duties of the Governor.

SEC. 75. Commissions and grants shall run in the name of the Commonwealth of Virginia, and be attested by the Governor, with the seal of the Commonwealth annexed.

SEC. 76. Every bill which shall have passed the Senate and House of Delegates, shall, before it becomes a law, be presented to the Governor. If he approve, he shall sign it; but, if not, he may return it with his objections to the house in which it originated, which shall enter the objections at large on its journal and proceed to reconsider the same. If, after such consideration, two-thirds of the members present, which two-thirds shall include a majority of the members elected to that house, shall agree to pass the bill it shall be sent, together with the objections, to the other house, by which it shall likewise be reconsidered, and if approved by two-thirds of all the members present, which two-thirds shall include a majority of the members elected to that house, it shall become a law, notwithstanding the objections. The Governor shall have the power to veto any particular item or items of an appropriation bill, but the veto shall not affect the item or items to which he does not object. The item or items objected to shall not take effect except in the manner heretofore provided in this section as to bills returned to the General Assembly without his approval. If he approve the general purpose of any bill, but disapprove any part or parts thereof, he may return it, with recommendations for its amendment, to the house in which it originated, whereupon the same proceedings shall be had in both houses upon the bill and his recommendations in relation to its amendment, as is above provided in relation to a bill which he shall have returned without his approval, and with his objections thereto: provided, that if after such reconsideration, both houses, by a vote of a majority of the members present in each, shall agree to amend the bill in accordance with his recommendations in relation thereto, or either house by such vote shall fail or refuse to so amend it, then, and in either case the bill shall be again sent to him, and he may act upon it as if it were then before him for the first time. But in all the cases above set forth the votes of both houses shall be determined by ayes and noes, and the names of the members voting for and against the bill, or item or items of an appropriation bill, shall be entered on the journal of each house. If any bill shall not be returned by the Governor within five days (Sunday excepted) after it shall have been presented to him, the same shall be a law in like manner as if he had signed it, unless the General Assembly shall, by final adjournment, prevent such return; in which case it shall be a law if approved by the Governor in the manner and to the extent above provided, within ten days after such adjournment, but not otherwise.

SEC. 77. A Lieutenant-Governor shall be elected at the same time and for the same term as the Governor, and his qualifications and the manner and ascertainment of his election, in all respects, shall be the same.

SEC. 78. In case of the removal of the Governor from office, or of his death, failure to qualify, resignation, removal from State, or inability to discharge the powers and duties of the office, the said office, with its compensation, shall devolve upon the Lieutenant-Governor; and the General Assembly shall provide by law for the discharge of the executive functions in other necessary cases.

SEC. 79. The Lieutenant-Governor shall be president of the Senate, but shall have no vote except in case of an equal division; and while acting as such, shall receive a compensation equal to that allowed to the Speaker of the House of Delegates.

SEC. 80. A Secretary of the Commonwealth shall be elected by the qualified voters of the State at the same time and for the same term as the Governor; and the fact of his election shall be ascertained as in the case of the Governor. He shall keep a daily record of the official acts of the Governor, which shall be signed by the Governor and attested by the Secretary, and, when required, he shall lay the same, and any papers, minutes and vouchers pertaining to his office, before either house of the General Assembly. He shall discharge such other duties as may be prescribed By law. All fees received by the Secretary of the Commonwealth shall be paid into the treasury monthly.

SEC. 81. A State Treasurer shall be elected by the qualified voters of the State at the same time and for the same term as the Governor; and the fact of his election shall be ascertained in the same manner. His powers and duties shall be prescribed by law.

SEC. 82. An Auditor of Public Accounts shall be elected by the joint vote of the two houses of the General Assembly for the term of four years. His powers and duties shall be prescribed by law.

SEC. 83. The salary of each officer of the Executive Department, except in those cases where the salary is determined by this Constitution, shall be fixed by law; and the salary of no such officer shall be increased or diminished during the term for which he shall have been elected or appointed.

SEC. 84. The General Assembly shall provide by law for the establishment and maintenance of an efficient system of checks and balances between the officers at the seat of government entrusted with the collection, receipt, custody, or disbursement of the revenues of the State.

SEC. 85. All State officers, and their deputies, assistants or employees, charged with the collection, custody, handling or disbursement of public funds, shall be required to give bond for the faithful performance of such duties; the amount of such bond in each case, and the manner in which security shall be furnished, to be specified and regulated by law.

SEC. 86. The General Assembly shall have power to establish and maintain a Bureau of Labor and Statistics, under such regulations as may be prescribed by law.

ARTICLE VI.
JUDICIARY DEPARTMENT.

SEC. 87. The Judiciary Department shall consist of a Supreme Court of Appeals, circuit courts, city courts, and such other courts as are hereinafter authorized. The jurisdiction of these tribunals and the judges thereof, except so far as conferred by this Constitution, shall be regulated by law.

SEC. 88. The Supreme Court of Appeals shall consist of five judges, any three of whom may hold a court. It shall have original jurisdiction in cases of habeas corpus, mandamus, and prohibition; but in all other cases, in which it shall have jurisdiction, it shall have appellate jurisdiction only.

Subject to such reasonable rules, as may be prescribed by law, as to the course of appeal, the limitation as to time, the security required, if any, the granting or refusing of appeals, and the procedure therein, it shall, by virtue of this Constitution, have appellate jurisdiction in all cases involving the constitutionality of a law as being repugnant to the Constitution of this State or of the United States, or involving the life or liberty of any person; and it shall also have appellate jurisdiction in such other cases, within the limits hereinafter denned, as may be prescribed by law; but no appeal shall be allowed to the Commonwealth in any case involving the life or liberty of a person, except that an appeal by the Commonwealth may be allowed by law in any case involving the violation of a law relating to the state revenue. No bond shall be required of any accused person as a condition of appeal, but a supersedeas bond may be required where the only punishment imposed in the court below is a fine.

The court shall not have jurisdiction in civil cases where the matter in controversy, exclusive of costs and of interest accrued since the judgment in the court below, is less in value or amount than three hundred dollars, except in controversies concerning the title to, or boundaries of land, the condemnation of property, the probate of a will, the appointment or qualification of a personal representative, guardian, committee, or curator, or concerning a mill, roadway, ferry, or landing, or the right of the State, county, or municipal corporation, to levy tolls or taxes, or involving the construction of any statute, ordinance or county proceeding imposing taxes; and, except in cases of habeas corpus, mandamus, and prohibition, the constitutionality of a law, or some other matter not merely pecuniary. After the year nineteen hundred and ten the General Assembly may change the jurisdiction of the court in matters merely pecuniary. The assent of at least three of the judges shall be required for the court to determine that any law is, or is not, repugnant to the Constitution of this State or of the United States; and if, in a case involving the constitutionality of any such law, not more than two of the judges sitting agree in opinion on the constitutional question involved, and the case cannot be determined, without passing on such question, no decision shall be rendered therein, but the case shall be reheard by a full court; and in no case where the jurisdiction of the court depends solely upon the fact that the constitutionality of a law is involved, shall the court decide the ease upon its merits, unless the contention of the appellant upon the constitutional question be sustained. Whenever the requisite majority of the judges sitting are unable to agree upon a decision, the case shall be reheard by a full bench, and any vacancy caused by any one or more of the judges being unable, unwilling, or disqualified to sit, shall be temporarily filled in a manner to be prescribed by law.

SEC. 89. The General Assembly may, from time to time, provide for a Special Court of Appeals to try any cases on the docket of the Supreme Court of Appeals in respect to which a majority of the judges are so situated as to make it improper for them to sit; and also to try any cases on said docket which cannot be disposed of with convenient dispatch. The said special court shall be composed of not less than three nor more than five of the judges of the circuit courts and city courts of record in cities of the first class, or of the judges of either of said courts, or of any of the judges of said courts together with one or more of the judges of the Supreme Court of Appeals.

SEC. 90. When a judgment or decree is reversed or affirmed by the Supreme Court of Appeals the reasons therefor shall be stated in writing and preserved with the record of the case.

SEC. 91. The judges of the Supreme Court of Appeals shall be chosen by the joint vote of the two houses of the General Assembly. They shall, when chosen, have held a judicial station in the United States, or shall have practiced law in this or some other state for five years. At the first election under this Constitution, the General Assembly shall elect the judges for terms of four, six, eight, ten, and twelve years respectively; and thereafter they shall be elected for terms of twelve years.

SEC. 92. The officers of the Supreme Court of Appeals shall be appointed by the court or by the judges in vacation. Their duties, compensation, and tenure of office shall be prescribed by law.

SEC. 93. The Supreme Court of Appeals shall hold its sessions at two or more places in the State, to be fixed by law.

SEC. 94. The State shall be divided into twenty-four judicial circuits, as follows:

The counties of Norfolk, Princess Anne, and the city of Portsmouth, shall constitute the first circuit.

The counties of Nansemond, Southampton, Isle of Wight, and the city of Norfolk, shall constitute the second circuit.

The counties of Prince George, Surry, Sussex, Greenesville, and Brunswick, shall constitute the third circuit.

The counties of Chesterfield, Powhatan, Dinwiddie, Nottoway, and Amelia, and the city of Petersburg, shall constitute the fourth circuit.

The counties of Prince Edward, Cumberland, Buckingham, Appomattox, and Charlotte, shall constitute the fifth circuit.

The counties of Lunenburg, Mecklenburg, Halifax, Campbell, and the city of Lynchburg, shall constitute the sixth circuit.

The counties of Pittsylvania, Franklin, Henry, and Patrick, and the city of Danville, shall constitute the seventh circuit.

The counties of Amherst, Nelson, Albemarle, Fluvanna, and Coochland, shall constitute the eighth circuit.

The counties of Rappahannock, Culpeper, Madison, Greene, Orange, and Louisa, shall constitute the ninth circuit.

The county of Henrico and the city of Richmond, shall constitute the tenth circuit.

Civil Government of Virginia 131

The counties of Accomac, Northampton, Elizabeth City, and the city of Newport News, shall constitute the eleventh circuit.

The counties of Richmond, Northumberland, Westmoreland, Lancaster, and Essex, shall constitute the twelfth circuit.

The counties of Gloucester, Mathews, King and Queen, King William, and Middlesex, shall constitute the thirteenth circuit.

The counties of New Kent, Charles City, York, Warwick, James City, and the city of Williamsburg, shall constitute the fourteenth circuit.

The counties of King George, Stafford, Spotsylvania, Caroline, and Hanover, shall constitute the fifteenth circuit.

The counties of Fauquier, Loudoun, Prince William, Fairfax, and Alexandria, and the city of Alexandria, shall constitute the sixteenth circuit.

The counties of Frederick, Clarke, Warren, Shenandoah, and Page, shall constitute the seventeenth circuit.

The counties of Rockingham, Augusta, and Rockbridge, shall constitute the eighteenth circuit.

The counties of Highland, Bath, Alleghany, Craig, and Botecourt, shall constitute the nineteenth circuit.

The counties of Bedford, Roanoke, Montgomery, and Floyd, and the city of Roanoke, shall constitute the twentieth circuit.

The counties of Pulaski, Carroll, Wythe, and Grayson, shall constitute the twenty-first circuit.

The counties of Bland, Tazewell, Giles, and Buchanan, shall constitute the twenty-second circuit.

The counties of Washington, Russell, and Smyth, shall constitute the twenty-third circuit.

The counties of Scott, Lee, Wise, and Dickenson, shall constitute the twenty-fourth circuit.

SEC. 95. After the first day of January, nineteen hundred and six, as the public interest requires, the General Assembly may rearrange the said circuits and increase or diminish the number thereof. But no new circuit shall be created containing, by the last United States census or other census provided by law, less than forty thousand inhabitants, nor when the effect of creating it will be to reduce the number of inhabitants in any existing circuit below forty thousand according to such census.

SEC. 96. For each circuit a judge shall be chosen by the joint vote of the two houses of the General Assembly. He shall when chosen, possess the same qualifications as judges of the Supreme Court of Appeals, and during his continuance in office shall reside in the circuit of which he is judge. At the first election under this Constitution, the General Assembly shall elect, as nearly as practicable, one fourth of the entire number of judges for terms of two years, one fourth for four years, one fourth for six years, and the remaining fourth for eight years, respectively, and thereafter they shall be elected for terms of eight years.

SEC 97 The number of terms of the circuit courts to be held for each county and city, shall be prescribed by law. But no separate circuit court shall be held for any city of the second class, until the city shall abolish its existing city court. The judge of one circuit may be required or authorized to hold court in any other circuit or city.

SEC 98 For the purposes of a judicial system, the cities of the State shall be divided into two classes. All cities shall belong to the first class which contain, as shown by the last United States census or other census provided by law, ten thousand inhabitants or more, and all cities shall belong to the second class which contain, as thus shown, less than ten thousand inhabitants. In each city of the first class, there shall be, in addition to the circuit court, a corporation court. In any city containing thirty thousand inhabitants or more, the General Assembly may provide for such additional courts as the public interest may require, and in every such city the city courts, as they now exist, shall continue until otherwise provided by law. In every city of the second class, the corporation or hustings court existing, at the time this Constitution goes into effect, shall continue hereafter under the name of the corporation court of such city, but it may be abolished by a vote of a majority of the qualified electors of such city, at an election held for the purpose, and whenever the office of judge of a corporation or hustings court of a city of the second class, whose salary is less than eight hundred dollars, shall become and remain vacant for ninety days consecutively, such court shall thereby cease to exist. In case of the abolition of the corporation or hustings court of any city of the second class, such city shall thereupon come in every respect within the jurisdiction of the circuit court of the county wherein it is situated, until otherwise provided by law, and the records of such corporation or hustings court shall thereupon become a part of the records of such circuit court, and be transferred thereto, and remain therein until otherwise provided by law, and during the existence of the corporation or hustings court, the circuit court of the county in which such city is situated, shall have concurrent jurisdiction with said corporation or hustings court in all actions at law and suits in equity.

SEC 99 For each city court of record a judge shall be chosen by the joint vote of the two houses of the General Assembly. He shall, when chosen, possess the same qualifications as judges of the Supreme Court of Appeals, and during his continuance in office shall reside within the jurisdiction of the court over which he presides, but the judge of the corporation court of any corporation having a city charter, and less than five thousand inhabitants, may reside outside its corporate limits; and the same person may be judge of such corporation court and judge of the corporation court of some other city having less than ten thousand inhabitants. At the first election of said judges under this Constitution, the General Assembly shall elect, as nearly as practicable, one-fourth of the entire number for terms of two years, one-fourth for four years, one-fourth for six years, and the remaining fourth for eight years; and thereafter they shall be elected for terms of eight years. The judges of city courts in cities of the first class may be required or authorized to hold the circuit courts of any county and the circuit courts of any city.

SEC. 100. The General Assembly shall have power to establish such court or courts of land registration as it may deem proper for the administration of any law it may adopt for the purpose of the settlement, registration, transfer, or assurance of titles to land in the State, or any part thereof.

SEC. 101. The General Assembly shall have power to confer upon the clerks of the several circuit courts jurisdiction, to be exercised in the manner and under the regulations to be prescribed by law, in the matter of the admission of wills to probate, and of the appointment and qualification of guardians, personal representatives, curators, appraisers, and committees of the estates of persons who have been adjudged insane or convicted of felony, and in the matter of the substitution of trustees.

SEC. 102. All the judges shall be commissioned by the Governor. They shall receive such salaries and allowances as may be determined by law within the limitations fixed by this Constitution, the amount of which shall not be increased or diminished during their terms of office. Their terms of office shall commence on the first day of February next following their election, and whenever a vacancy occurs in the office of judge, his successor shall be elected for the unexpired term.

SEC. 103. The salaries of the judges of the Supreme Court of Appeals shall be not less than four thousand dollars per annum, and shall be paid by the State.

The salary of the judge of each circuit court shall be not less than two thousand dollars per annum, one-half of which shall be paid by the State, the other half by the counties and cities composing the circuit, according to their respective population; except that of the salary of the judge of the circuit court of the city of Richmond, the State shall pay the proportion which would otherwise fall to the city of Richmond. The salary of a judge of a city court in a city of the first class shall be not less than two thousand dollars per annum, one-half of which shall be paid by the State, the other half by the city. The whole of the aforesaid salaries of said judges shall be paid out of the state treasury, the State to be reimbursed by the respective counties and cities. Any city may, by an ordinance, increase the salaries of its city or circuit judges, or any one or more of them as it may deem proper, and the increase shall be paid wholly by the city, but shall not be enlarged or diminished during the term of office of the judge. Each city containing less than ten thousand inhabitants shall pay the salary of the judge of its corporation or hustings court.

SEC. 104. Judges may be removed from office for cause, by a concurrent vote of both houses of the General Assembly; but a majority of all the members elected to each house must concur in such vote, and the cause of removal shall be entered on the journal of each house. The judge against whom the General Assembly may be about to proceed shall have notice thereof, accompanied by a copy of the causes alleged for his removal, at least twenty days before the day on which either house of the General Assembly shall act thereon.

SEC. 105. No judge of the Supreme Court of Appeals, of the circuit court, or of any city court of record shall practice law, within or without this State, nor shall he hold any other office of public-trust during his continuance in office; except that the judge of a corporation or hustings court in a city of the second class, may hold the office of commissioner in chancery of the circuit court for the county in which the city is located.

SEC. 106. Writs shall run in the name of the "Commonwealth of Virginia," and be attested by the clerks of the several courts. Indictments shall conclude "against the peace and dignity of the Commonwealth."

SEC. 107. An Attorney-General shall be elected by the qualified voters of the State at the same time and for the same term as the Governor; and the fact of his election shall be ascertained in the same manner. He shall be commissioned by the Governor, perform such duties and receive such compensation as may be prescribed by law, and shall be removable in the manner prescribed for the removal of judges.

SEC 108. The General Assembly shall provide for the appointment or election and for the jurisdiction of such justices of the peace as the public interest may require.

SEC. 109. The General Assembly shall provide by whom, and in what manner, applications for bail shall be heard and determined.

ARTICLE VII.
ORGANIZATION AND GOVERNMENT OF COUNTIES.

SEC. 110. There shall be elected by the qualified voters of each county, one county treasurer,--who shall not be elected or serve for more than two consecutive terms, nor act as deputy of his immediate successor; one sheriff, one attorney for the Commonwealth, and one county clerk, who shall be the clerk of the circuit court. There shall be elected or appointed, for four years, as the General Assembly may provide commissioners of the revenue, for each county, the number, duties and compensation of whom shall be prescribed by law; but should such commissioners of the revenue be chosen by election by the people then they shall be ineligibile for re-election to the office for the next succeeding term.

There shall be appointed for each county, in such manner as may be provided by law, one superintendent of the poor, and one county surveyor.

SEC. 111. The magisterial districts shall, until changed by law, remain as now constituted: provided, that hereafter no additional districts shall be made containing less than thirty square miles. In each district there shall be elected by the qualified voters thereof, one supervisor. The supervisors of the districts shall constitute the board of supervisors of the county, which shall meet at stated periods and at other times as often as may be necessary, lay the county and district levies, pass upon all claims against the county, subject to such appeal as may be provided by law, and perform such duties as may be required by law.

SEC. 112. All regular elections for county and district officers shall be held on Tuesday after the first Monday in November, and all of said officers shall enter upon the duties of their offices on the first day of January next succeeding their election, and shall hold their respective offices for the term of four years, except that the county clerk shall hold office for eight years; provided that the term of the clerks first elected under this Constitution shall begin on the first of February, nineteen hundred and four, and end on the first of January, nineteen hundred and twelve.

SEC. 113. No person shall at the same time hold more than one of the offices mentioned in this article. Any officer required by law to give bond may be required to give additional security thereon, or to execute a new bond, and in default of so doing his office shall be declared vacant.

SEC. 114, Counties shall not be made responsible for the acts of the sheriffs.

SEC. 115. The General Assembly shall provide for the examination of the books, accounts and settlements of county and city officers who are charged with the collection and disbursement of public funds.

ARTICLE VIII.
ORGANIZATION AND GOVERNMENT OF CITIES AND TOWNS.

SEC. 116. As used in this article the words "incorporated communities" shall be construed to relate only to cities and towns. All incorporated communities, having within defined boundaries a population of five thousand or more, shall be known as cities; and all incorporated communities having within defined boundaries a population of less than five thousand, shall be known as towns. In determining the population of such cities and towns the General Assembly shall be governed by the last United States census, or such other enumeration as may be made by authority of the General Assembly; but nothing in this section shall be construed to repeal the charter of any incorporated community of less than five thousand inhabitants having a city charter at the time of the adoption of this Constitution, or to prevent the abolition by such incorporated communities of the corporation or hustings court thereof.

SEC. 117. General laws for the organization and government of cities and towns shall be enacted by the General Assembly, and no special act shall be passed in relation thereto, except in the manner provided in Article Four of this Constitution, and then only by a recorded vote of two-thirds of the members elected to each house. But each of the cities and towns of the State having at the time of the adoption of this Constitution a municipal charter may retain the same, except so far as it shall be repealed or amended by the General Assembly: provided, that every such charter is hereby amended so as to conform to all the provisions, restrictions, limitations and powers set forth in this article, or otherwise provided in this Constitution.

SEC. 118. In each city which has a court in whose office deeds are admitted to record, there shall be elected for a term of eight years by the qualified voters of such city a clerk of said court, who shall perform such other duties as may be required by law.

There shall be elected in like manner and for a like term all such additional clerks of courts for cities as the General Assembly may prescribe, or as are now authorized by law, so long as such courts shall continue in existence. But in no city of less than thirty thousand inhabitants shall there be more than one clerk of the court, who shall be clerk of all the courts of record in such city.

SEC. 119. In every city, so long as it has a corporation court, or a separate circuit court, there shall be elected for a term of four years by the qualified voters of such city, one attorney for the Commonwealth, who shall also, in those cities having a separate circuit court, be the attorney for the Commonwealth, for such circuit court.

In every city there shall be elected, or appointed, for a term of four years, in a manner to be provided by law, one commissioner of revenue, whose duties and compensation shall be prescribed by law; but should he be elected by the people, he shall be ineligible for reelection to the office for the next succeeding term.

SEC. 120. In every city there shall be elected by the qualified voters thereof one city treasurer, for a term of four years, but he shall not be eligible for more than two consecutive terms, nor act as deputy for his immediate successor; one city sergeant, for a term of four years, whose duties shall be prescribed by law; and, a mayor, for a term of four years, who shall be the chief executive officer of such city. All city and town officers, whose election or appointment is not provided for by this Constitution, shall be elected by the electors of such cities and towns, or of some division thereof, or appointed by such authorities thereof as the General Assembly shall designate.

The mayor shall see that the duties of the various city officers, members of the police and fire departments, whether elected or appointed, in and for such city, are faithfully performed. He shall have power to investigate their acts, have access to all books and documents in their offices, and may examine them and their subordinates on oath. The evidence given by persons so examined shall not be used against them in any criminal proceedings. He shall also have power to suspend such officers and the members of the police and fire departments, and to remove such officers, and also such members of said departments when authorized by the General Assembly, for misconduct in office or neglect of duty, to be specified in the order of suspension or removal; but no such removal shall be made without reasonable notice to the officer complained of, and an opportunity afforded him to be heard in person, or by counsel, and to present testimony in his defense. From such order of suspension or removal, the city officer so suspended or removed shall have an appeal of right to the corporation court, or, if there be no such court, to the circuit court of such city, in which court the case shall be heard de novo by the judge thereof, whose decision shall be final. He shall have all other powers and duties which may be conferred and imposed upon him by general laws.

SEC. 121. There shall be in every city a council, composed of two branches having a different number of members, whose powers and terms of office shall be prescribed by law, and whose members shall be elected by the qualified voters of such city, in the manner prescribed by law, but so as to give as far as practicable, to each ward of such city, equal representation in each branch of said council in proportion to the population of such ward; but in cities of under ten thousand population the General Assembly may permit the council to consist of one branch. No member of the council shall be eligible during his tenure of office as such member, or for one year thereafter, to any office to be filled by the council by election or appointment. The council of every city may, in a manner prescribed by law, increase or diminish the number, and change the boundaries, of the wards thereof, and shall, in the year nineteen hundred and three, and in every tenth year thereafter, and also whenever the boundaries of such wards are changed, re-apportion the representation in the council among the wards in a manner prescribed by law; and whenever the council of any such city shall fail to perform the duty so prescribed, a mandamus shall lie on behalf of any citizen thereof to compel its performance.

SEC. 122. The mayors and councils of cities shall be elected on the second Tuesday in June, and their terms of office shall begin on the first day of September succeeding. All other elective officers, provided for by this article, or hereafter authorized by law, shall be elected on the Tuesday after the first Monday in November, and their terms of office shall begin on the first day of January succeeding, except that the terms of office of clerks of the city courts shall begin coincidently with that of the judges of said courts: provided, that the General Assembly may change the time of election of all or any of the said officers, except that the election and the beginning of the terms of mayors and councils of cities shall not be made by the General Assembly to occur at the same time with the election and beginning of the terms of office of the other elective officers provided for by this Constitution.

SEC. 123. Every ordinance, or resolution having the effect of an ordinance, shall, before it becomes operative, be presented to the mayor. If he approve he shall sign it, but if not, if the council consist of two branches, he may return it, with his objections in writing, to the clerk, or other recording officer, of that branch in which it originated; which branch shall enter the objections at length on its journal and proceed to reconsider it. If after such consideration two thirds of all the members elected thereto shall agree to pass the ordinance or resolution it shall be sent, together with the objections, to the other branch, by which it shall likewise be considered, and if approved by two thirds of all the members elected thereto, it shall become operative notwithstanding the objections of the mayor. But in all such cases the votes of both branches of the council shall be determined by yeas and nays, and the names of the members voting for and against the ordinance or resolution shall be entered on the journal of each branch. If the council consist of a single branch, the mayor's objections in wilting to any ordinance, or resolution having the effect of an ordinance, shall be returned to the clerk, or other recording officer of the council, and be entered at length on its journal, whereupon the council shall proceed to reconsider the same. Upon such consideration the vote shall be taken in the same manner as where the council consists of two branches, and if the ordinance or resolution be approved by two thirds of all the members elected to the council, it shall become operative notwithstanding the objections of the mayor. If any ordnance or resolution shall not be returned by the major within five days (Sunday excepted), after it shall have been presented to him, it shall become operative in like manner as if he had signed it, unless his term of office, or that of the council, shall expire within said five days.

The mayor shall have the power to veto any particular item or items of an appropriation, ordnance or resolution, but the veto shall not affect any item or items to which he does not object. The item or items objected to shall not take effect except in the manner provided in this section as to ordnances or resolutions not approved by the mayor. No ordinance or resolution appropriating money exceeding the sum of one hundred dollars, imposing taxes, or authorizing the borrowing of money, shall be passed, except by a recorded affirmative vote of a majority of all the members elected to the council or to each branch thereof where there are two, and in case of the veto by the mayor of such ordnance or resolution, it shall require a recorded affirmative vote of two thirds of all the members elected to the council, or to each branch thereof where there are two, to pass the same over such veto in the manner provided in this section. Nothing contained in this section shall operate to repeal or amend any provision in any existing city charter requiring a two thirds vote for the passage of any ordinance as to the appropriation of money, imposing taxes or authorizing the borrowing of money.

SEC. 124. No street, railway, gas, water, steam, or electric heating, electric light or power, cold storage, compressed air, viaduct, conduct telephone, or bridge, company, nor any corporation, association, person or partnership, engaged in these or like enterprises, shall be permitted to use the streets, alleys, or public grounds of a city or town without the previous consent of the corporate authorities of such city or town.

SEC. 125. The rights of no city or town in and to its water front, wharf property, public landings, wharves, docks, streets, avenues, parks, budges, and other public places, and its gas, water, and electric works shall be sold except by an ordinance or resolution passed by a recorded affirmative vote of three fourths of all the members elected to the council, or to each branch thereof where there are two, and under such other restrictions as may be imposed by law, and in case of the veto by the mayor of such an ordinance or resolution, it shall require a recorded affirmative vote of three fourths of all the members elected to the council, or to each branch thereof--where there are two, had in the manner heretofore provided for in this article, to pass the same over the veto. So franchise, lease or light of any kind to use any such public property or any other public property or easement of any description, in a manner not permitted to the general public, shall be granted for a longer period than thirty years. Before planting any such franchise or privilege for a term of years, except for a trunk railway, the municipality shall first, after due advertisement, reserve bids therefor publicly, in such manner as may be provided by law, and shall then act as may be required by law. Such grant, and any contract in pursuance thereof, may provide that upon the termination of the grant the plant as well as the property, if any, of the grantee in the streets, avenues, and other public places shall thereupon, without compensation to the grantee, or upon the payment of a fair valuation therefor, be and become the property of the said city or town, but the grantee shall be entitled to no payment by reason of the value of the franchise, and any such plant or property acquired by a city or town may be sold or leased, or, if authorized by law, maintained, controlled and operated, by such city or town. Every such grant shall specify the mode of determining any valuation therein provided for, and shall make adequate provision by way of forfeiture of the grant, or otherwise, to secure efficiency of public service at reasonable rates, and the maintenance of the property in good order throughout the term of the grant. Nothing herein contained shall be construed as preventing the General Assembly from prescribing additional restrictions on the powers of cities and towns in granting franchises or in selling or leasing any of their property, or as repealing any additional restriction now required in relation thereto in any existing municipal charter.

SEC. 126. The General Assembly shall provide by general laws for the extension and the contraction, from time to time, of the corporate limits of cities and towns, and no special act for such purpose shall be valid.

SEC. 127. No city or town shall issue any bonds or other interest bearing obligations for any purpose, or in any manner, to an amount which, including existing indebtedness, shall, at any time, exceed eighteen per centum of the assessed valuation of the real estate in the city or town subject to taxation, as shown by the last preceding assessment for taxes provided, however that nothing above contained in this section shall apply to those cities and towns whose charters existing at the adoption of this Constitution authorize a larger percentage of indebtedness than is authorized by this section and provided further, that in determining the limitation of the power of a city or town to incur indebtedness there shall not be included the following classes of indebtedness

(a.) Certificates of indebtedness, revenue bonds or other obligations issued in anticipation of the collection of the revenue of such city or town for the then current year; provided that such certificates, bonds or other obligations mature within one year from the date of their issue, and be not past due, and do not exceed the revenue for such year;

(b.) Bonds authorized by an ordinance enacted in accordance with section One

Hundred and Twenty-three, and approved by the affirmative vote of the majority of the qualified voters of the city or town voting upon the question of their issuance, at the general election next succeeding the enactment of the ordinance, or at a special election held for that purpose, for a supply of water or other specific undertaking from which the city or town may derive a revenue; but from and after a period to be determined by the council, not exceeding five years from the date of such election, whenever and for so long as such undertaking fails to produce sufficient revenue to pay for cost of operation and administration (including interest on bonds issued therefor, and the cost of insurance against loss by injury to persons or property), and an annual amount to be covered into a sinking fund sufficient to pay, at or before maturity, all bonds issued on account of said undertaking, all such bonds outstanding shall be included in determining the limitation of the power to incur indebtedness, unless the principal and interest thereof be made payable exclusively from the receipts of the undertaking.

SEC. 128. In cities and towns the assessment of real estate and personal property for the purpose of muicipal taxation, shall be the same as the assessment thereof for the purpose of state taxation, whenever there shall be a state assessment of such property.

ARTICLE IX.
EDUCATION AND PUBLIC INSTRUCTION.

SEC. 129. The General Assembly shall establish and maintain an efficient system of public free schools throughout the State.

SEC. 130. The general supervision of the school system shall be vested in a State Board of Education, composed of the Governor, Attorney-General, Superintendent of Public Instruction, and three experienced educators to be elected quadrennially by the Senate, from a list of eligibles, consisting of one from each of the faculties, and nominated by the respective boards of visitors or trustees, of the University of Virginia, the Virginia Military Institute, the Virginia Polytechnic Institute, the State Female Normal School at Farmville, the School for the Deaf and Blind, and also of the College of William and Mary, so long as the State continue its annual appropriation to the last named institution.

The board thus constituted shall select and associate with itself two division superintendents of schools, one from a county and the other from a city, who shall hold office for two years, and whose powers and duties shall be identical with those of other members, except that they shall not participate in the appointment of any public school official.

Any vacancy occurring during the term of any member of the board shall be filled for the unexpired term by said board.

SEC. 131. The Superintendent of Public Instruction, who shall be an experienced educator, shall be elected by the qualified voters of the State at the same time and for the same term as the Governor. Any vacancy in said office shall be filled for the unexpired term by the said board.

His duties shall be prescribed by the State Board of Education, of which he shall be ex-officio president; and his compensation shall be fixed by law.

SEC. 132. The duties and powers of the State Board of Education shall be as follows:

First. It may, in its discretion, divide the State into appropriate school divisions, comprising not less than one county or city each, but no county or city shall be divided in the formation of such divisions. It shall, subject to the confirmation of the Senate, appoint, for each of such divisions, one superintendent of schools, who shall hold office for four years, and shall prescribe his duties, and may remove him for cause and upon notice.

Second. It shall have, regulated by law, the management and investment of the school fund.

Third. It shall have authority to make all needful rules and regulations for the management and conduct of the schools, which, when published and distributed, shall have the force and effect of law, subject to the authority of the General Assembly to revise, amend, or repeal the same.

Fourth. It shall select text books and educational appliances for vise in the schools of the State, exercising such discretion as it may see fit in the selection of books suitable for the schools in the cities and counties respectively.

Fifth. It shall appoint a board of directors, consisting of five members, to serve without compensation, which shall have the management of the State Library, and the appointment of a librarian and other employees thereof, subject to such rules and regulations as the General Assembly snail prescribe; but the Supreme Court of Appeals shall have the management of the law library and the appointment of the librarian and other employees thereof.

SEC. 133. Each magisterial district shall constitute a separate school district, unless otherwise provided by law. In each school district there shall be three trustees selected, in the manner and for the term of office prescribed by law.

SEC. 134. The General Assembly shall set apart as a permanent and perpetual literary fund, the present literary fund of the State; the proceeds of all public lands donated by Congress for public free school purposes; of all escheated property; of all waste and unappropriated lands; of all property accruing to the State by forfeiture, and all fines collected for offences committed against the State, and such other sums as the General Assembly may apppropriate.

SEC. 135. The General Assembly shall apply the annual interest on the literary fund; that portion of the capitation tax provided for in the Constitution to be paid into the state treasury, and not returnable to the counties and cities; and an annual tax on property of not less than one nor more than five mills on the dollar to the schools of the primary and grammar grades, for the equal benefit of all of the people of the State, to be apportioned on a basis of school population; the number of children between the ages of seven and twenty years in each school district to be the basis of such apportionment: but if at any time the several kinds or classes of property shall be segregated for the purposes of taxation, so as to specify and determine upon what subjects state taxes and upon what subjects local taxes may be levied, then the General Assembly may otherwise provide for a fixed appropriation of state revenue to the support of the schools not less than that provided in this section.

SEC. 136. Each county, city, town if the same be a separate school district, and school district is authorized to raise additional sums by a tax on property, not to exceed in the aggregate five mills on the dollar in any one year, to be apportioned and expended by the local school authorities of said counties, cities, towns and district in establishing and maintaining such schools as in their judgment the public welfare may require: provided, that such primary schools as may be established in any school year, shall be maintained at least four months of that school year, before any part of the fund assessed and collected may be devoted to the establishment of schools of higher grade. The boards of supervisors of the several counties, and the councils of the several cities, and towns if the same be separate schools districts, shall provide for the levy and collection of such local school taxes.

SEC. 137. The General Assembly may establish agricultural, normal, manual training and technical schools, and such grades of schools as shall be for the public good.

SEC. 138. The General Assembly may, in its discretion, provide for the compulsory education of children between the ages of eight and twelve years, except such as are weak in body or mind, or can read and write, or are attending private schools, or are excused for cause by the district school trustees.

SEC. 139. Provision shall be made to supply children attending the public schools with necessary text-books in cases where the parent or guardian is unable, by reason of poverty, to furnish them.

SEC. 140. White and colored children shall not be taught in the same school.

SEC. 141. No appropriation of public funds shall be made to any school or institution of learning not owned or exclusively controlled by the State or some political subdivision thereof: provided, first, that the General Assembly may, in its discretion, continue the appropriations to the College of William and Mary; second, that this section shall not be construed as requiring or prohibiting the continuance or discontinuance by the General Assembly of the payment of interest on certain bonds held by certain schools and colleges as provided by an act of the General Assembly, approved February twenty-third, eighteen hundred and ninety-two, relating to bonds held by schools and colleges; third, that counties, cities, towns, and districts may make appropriations to non-sectarian schools of manual, industrial, or technical training, and also to any school or institution of learning owned or exclusively controlled by such county, city, town, or school district.

SEC. 142. Members of the boards of visitors or trustees of educational institutions shall be appointed as may be provided by law, and shall hold for the term of four years: provided, that at the first appointment, if the board be of an even number, one-half of them, or, if of an odd number, the least majority of them, shall be appointed for two years.

ARTICLE X.
AGRICULTURE AND IMMIGRATION.

SEC. 143. There shall be a Department of Agriculture and Immigration, which shall be permanently maintained at the capital of the State, and which shall be under the management and control of a Board of Agriculture and Immigration, composed of one member from each congressional district, who shall be a practical farmer, appointed by the Governor for a term of four years, subject to confirmation by the Senate, and the president of the Virginia Polytechnic Institute, who shall be ex-officio a member of the board: provided, that members of the board first appointed under this Constitution from the congressional districts bearing odd numbers shall hold office for two years.

SEC. 144. The powers and duties of the board shall be prescribed by law: provided, that it shall have power to elect and remove its officers, and establish elsewhere in the State subordinate branches of said department.

SEC. 145. There shall be a Commissioner of Agriculture and Immigration, whose term of office shall be four years, and who shall be elected by the qualified voters of the State, and whose powers and duties shall be prescribed by the Board of Agriculture and Immigration until otherwise provided by law.

SEC. 146. The president of the Board of Agriculture and Immigration shall be ex-officio a member of the Board of Visitors of the Virginia Polytechnic Institute.

ARTICLE XI
PUBLIC INSTITUTIONS AND PRISONS.

SEC. 147. There shall be a state penitentiary,--with such branch prisons and prison farms as may be provided by law.

SEC. 148. There shall be appointed by the Governor, subject to confirmation by the Senate, a board of five directors which, subject to such regulations and requirements as may be prescribed by law, shall have the government and control of the penitentiary, branch prisons, and prison farms, and shall appoint the superintendents and surgeons thereof. The respective superintendents shall appoint, and may remove, all other officers and employees of the penitentiary, branch prisons, and prison farms, subject to the approval of the board of directors. The superintendents and surgeons shall be appointed for a term of four years, and be removable by the board of directors for misbehavior, incapacity, neglect of official duty, or acts performed without authority of law. The terms of the directors first appointed shall be one, two, three, four, and five years respectively; and thereafter, upon the expiration of the term of a director, his successor shall be appointed for a term of five years.

SEC. 149. For each state hospital for the insane now existing, or hereafter established, there shall be a special board of directors, consisting of three members, who shall be appointed by the Governor, subject to confirmation by the Senate; such board shall have the management of the hospital for which it is appointed, under the supervision and control of the general board of directors hereinafter constituted. The terms of the directors first appointed shall be two, four, and six years, respectively, and thereafter, upon the expiration of the term of a member, his successor shall be appointed for a term of six years.

SEC. 150. There shall be a general board of directors for the control and management of all the state hospitals for the insane now existing or hereafter established, which shall consist of all the directors appointed members of the several special boards. The general board of directors shall be subject to such regulations and requirements as the General Assembly may from time to time prescribe, and shall have full power and control over the special boards of directors and all of the officers and employees of the said hospitals.

SEC. 151. The general board of directors shall appoint for a term of four years a superintendent for each hospital, who shall be removable by said board for misbehavior, incapacity, neglect of official duty, or acts performed without authority of law. The special board of each hospital, shall, subject to the approval of the general board, appoint for a term of four years all other resident officers. The superintendent of each hospital shall appoint, and may remove, with the approval of the special board, all other employees of such hospital.

SEC. 152. There shall be a Commissioner of State Hospitals for the Insane, who shall be appointed by the Governor, subject to confirmation by the Senate, for a term of four years. He shall be ex-officio chairman of the general and of each of the special boards of directors, and shall be responsible for the proper disbursement of all moneys appropriated or received from any source for the maintenance of such hospitals; he shall cause to be established and maintained at all of the hospitals a uniform system of keeping the records and the accounts of money received and disbursed and of making reports thereof. He shall perform such other duties and shall execute such bond and receive such salary as may be prescribed by law.

ARTICLE XII.
CORPORATIONS.

SEC. 153. As used in this article, the term "corporation" or "company" shall include all trusts, associations and joint stock companies having any powers or privileges not possessed by individuals or unlimited partnerships, and exclude all municipal corporations and public institutions owned or controlled by the State; the term "charter" shall be construed to mean the charter of incorporation by, or under, which any such corporation is formed; the term "transportation company" shall include any company, trustee, or other person owning, leasing or operating for hire a railroad, street railway, canal, steamboat or steamship line, and also any freight car company, car association, or car trust, express company, or company, trustee or person in any way engaged in business as a common carrier over a route acquired in whole or in part under the right of eminent domain; the term "rate" shall be construed to mean "rate of charge for any service rendered or to be rendered"; the terms "rate," "charge" and "regulation," shall include joint rates, joint charges, and joint regulations, respectively; the term "transmission company" shall include any company owning, leasing, or operating for hire, any telegraph or telephone line; the term "freight" shall be construed to mean any property transported, or received for transportation, by any transportation company; the term "public service corporation" shall include all transportation and transmission companies, all gas, electric light, heat and power companies, and all persons authorized to exercise the right of eminent domain, or to use or occupy any street, alley or public highway, whether along, over, or under the same, in a manner not permitted to the general public; the term "person," as used in this article, shall include individuals, partnerships and corporations, in the singular as well as plural number; the term "bond" shall mean all certificates, or written evidences, of indebtedness issued by any corporation and secured by mortgage or trust deed; the term "frank" shall be construed to mean any writing or token, issued by, or under authority of, a transmission company, entitling the holder to any service from such company free of charge. The provisions of this article shall always be so restricted in their application as not to conflict with any of the provisions of the Constitution of the United States, and as if the necessary limitations upon their interpretation had been herein expressed in each case.

SEC. 154. The creation of corporations, and the extension and amendment of charters (whether heretofore or hereafter granted), shall be provided for by general laws, and no charter shall be granted, amended or extended by special act, nor shall authority in such matters be conferred upon any tribunal or officer, except to ascertain whether the applicants have, by complying with the requirements of the law, entitled themselves to the charier, amendment or extension applied for, and to issue, or refuse, the same accordingly. Such general laws may be amended or repealed by the General Assembly; and all charters and amendments of charters, now existing and revocable, or hereafter granted or extended, may be repealed at any time by special act. Provision shall be made, by general laws, for the voluntary surrender of its charter by any corporation, and for the forfeiture thereof for non-user or mis- user. The General Assembly shall not, by special act, regulate the affairs of any corporation, nor, by such act, give it any rights, powers or privileges.

SEC. 155. A permanent commission, to consist of three members, is hereby created, which shall be known as the State Corporation Commission. The commissioners shall be appointed by the Governor, subject to confirmation by the General Assembly in joint session, and their regular terms of office shall be six years, respectively, except those first appointed under this Constitution, of whom, one shall be appointed to hold office until the first day of February, nineteen hundred and four, one, until the first day of February, nineteen hundred and six, and one, until the first day of February, nineteen hundred and eight. Whenever a vacancy in the commission shall occur, the Governor shall forthwith appoint a qualified person to fill the same for the unexpired term, subject to confirmation by the General Assembly as aforesaid Commissioners appointed for regular terms shall, at the beginning of the terms for which appointed, and those appointed to fill vacancies shall, immediately upon their appointments, enter upon the duties of their office, but no person so appointed, either for a regular term, or to fill a vacancy, shall enter upon, or continue in, office after the General Assembly shall have refused to confirm his appointment, or adjourned sine die without confirming the same, nor shall he be eligible for reappointment to fill the vacancy caused by such refusal or failure to confirm. No person while employed by, or holding any office in relation to, any transportation or transmission company, or while in any wise financially interested therein, or while engaged in practicing law, shall hold office as a member of said commission, or perform any of the duties thereof. At least one of the commissioners shall have the qualifications prescribed for judges of the Supreme Court of Appeals, and any commissioner may be impeached or removed in the manner provided for the impeachment or removal of a judge of said court. The commission shall annually elect one of their members chairman of the same, and shall have one clerk, one bailiff and such other clerks, officers, assistants and subordinates as may be provided by law, all of whom shall be appointed, and subject to removal, by the commission. It shall prescribe its own rules of order and procedure, except so far as the same are specified in this Constitution or any amendment thereof. The General Assembly may establish within the department, and subject to the supervision and control, of the commission, subordinate divisions, or bureaus, of insurance, banking or other special branches of the business of that department. All sessions of the commission shall be public, and a permanent record shall be kept of all its judgments, rules, orders, findings and decisions, and of all reports made to, or by, it. Two of the commissioners shall constitute a quorum for the transaction of business, whether there be a vacancy in the commission or not. The commission shall keep its office open for business on every day except Sundays and legal holidays. Transportation companies shall at all times transport, free of charge, within this State, the members of said commission and its officers, or any of them, when engaged on their official duties. The General Assembly shall provide suitable quarters for the commission and funds for its lawful expenses, including pay for witnesses summoned, and costs of executing processes issued, by the commission of its own motion, and shall fix the salaries of the members, clerks, assistants and subordinates of the commission and provide for the payment thereof, but the salary of each commissioner shall not be less than four thousand dollars per annum After the first day of January, nineteen hundred and eight, the General Assembly may provide for the election of the members of the commission by the qualified voters of the State, in which event, vacancies thereafter occurring shall be filled as here inbefore provided, until the expiration of twenty days after the next general election, held not less than sixty days after the vacancy occurs, at which election the vacancy shall be filled for the residue of the unexpired term

SEC 156 (a) Subject to the provisions of this Constitution and to such requirements, rules and regulations as may be prescribed by law, the State Corporation Commission shall be the department of government through which shall be issued all charters and amendments or extensions thereof, for domestic corporations, and all licenses to do business in this State to foreign corporations, and through which shall be carried out all the provisions of this Constitution, and of the laws made in pursuance thereof, for the creation, visitation, supervision, regulation and control of corporations chartered by, or doing business in, this State The commission shall prescribe the forms of all reports which may be required of such corporations by this Constitution or by law, it shall collect, receive, and preserve such reports, and annually tabulate and publish them in statistical form, it shall have all the rights and powers of, and perform all the duties devolving upon, the Railroad Commissioner and the Board of Public Works, at the time this Constitution goes into effect, except so far as they are inconsistent with this Constitution, or may be hereafter abolished or changed by law

(b) The commission shall have the power, and be charged with the duty, of supervising, regulating and controlling all transportation and transmission companies doing business in this State, in all matters relating to the performance of their public duties and their charges therefor, and of correcting abuses therein by such companies, and to that end the commission shall, from time to time prescribe, and enforce against such companies, in the manner hereinafter authorized, such rates, charges, classifications of traffic, and rules and regulations, and shall require them to establish and maintain all such public service, facilities and conveniences, as may be reasonable and just, which said rates, charges, classifications, rules, regulations and requirements, the commission may, from time to time, alter or amend. All rates, charges, classifications, rules and regulations adopted, or acted upon, by any such company, inconsistent with those prescribed by the commission, within the scope of its authority, shall be unlawful and void. The commission shall also have the right at all times to inspect the books and papers of all transportation and transmission companies doing business in this State, and to require from such companies, from time to time, special reports and statements under oath concerning their business, it shall keep itself fully informed of the physical condition of all the railroads of the State, as to the manner in which they are operated, with reference to the security and accommodation of the public, and shall, from time to time, make and enforce such requirements, rules and regulations as may be necessary to prevent unjust or unreasonable discriminations by any transportation or transmission company in favor of, or against, any person, locality, community, connecting line, or kind of traffic, in the matter of car service, train or boat schedule, efficiency of transportation or otherwise, in connection with the public duties of such company Before the commission shall prescribe or fix any rate, charge, or classification of traffic, and before it shall make any order, rule, regulation or requirement directed against any one or more companies by name, the company or companies to be affected by such rate, charge, classification, order, rule, regulation or requirement, shall first be given, by the commission, at least ten days' notice of the time and place, when and where the contemplated action in the premises will be considered and disposed of, and shall be afforded a reasonable opportunity to introduce evidence and to be heard thereon, to the end that justice may be done, and shall have process to enforce the attendance of witnesses, and before the commission shall make or prescribe any general order, rule, regulation or requirement, not directed against any specific company or companies by name, the contemplated general order, rule, regulation or requirement shall first be published in substance, not less than once a week for four consecutive weeks in one or more of the newspapers of general circulation published in the city of Richmond, Virginia, together with notice of the time and place, when and where the commission will hear any objections which may be urged by any person interested, against the proposed order, rule, regulation or requirement, and every such general order, rule, regulation or requirement, made by the commission shall be published at length, for the time and in the manner above specified, before it shall go into effect, and shall also, as long as it remains in force, be published in each subsequent annual report of the commission. The authority of the commission (subject to review on appeal as hereinafter provided) to prescribe rates, charges and classifications of traffic, for transportation and transmission companies, shall be paramount, but its authority to prescribe any other rules, regulations or requirements for corporations or other persons shall be subject to the superior authority of the General Assembly to legislate thereon by general laws provided, however, that nothing in this section shall impair the right which has heretofore been, or may hereafter be, conferred by law upon the authorities of any city, town or county to prescribe rules, regulations or rates of charge to be observed by any public service corporation in connection with any services performed by it under a municipal or county franchise granted by such city, town or county, so far as such services may be wholly within the limits of the city, town or county granting the franchise. Upon the request of the parties interested, it shall be the duty of the commission, as far as possible, to effect, by mediation, the adjustment of claims, and the settlement of controversies, between transportation or transmission companies and their patrons

(c) In all matters pertaining to the public visitation, regulation or control of corporations, and within the jurisdiction of the commission, it shall have the powers and authority of a court of record, to administer oaths, to compel the attendance of witnesses and the production of papers, to punish for contempt any person guilty of disrespectful or disorderly conduct in the presence of the commission while in session, and to enforce compliance with any of its lawful orders or requirements by adjudging and enforcing by its own appropriate process, against the delinquent or offending company (after it shall have been first duly cited, proceeded against by due process of law before the commission sitting as a court, and afforded opportunity to introduce evidence and to be heard, as well against the validity, justness or reasonableness of the order or requirement alleged to have been violated, as against the liability of the company for the alleged violation), such fines or other penalties as may be prescribed or authorized by this Constitution or by law. The commission may be vested with such additional powers, and charged with such other duties (not inconsistent with this Constitution) as may be prescribed by law, in connection with the visitation, regulation or control of corporations, or with the prescribing and enforcing of rates and charges to be observed in the conduct of any business where the State has the right to prescribe the rates and charges in connection therewith, or with the assessment of the property of corporations or the appraisement of their franchises, for taxation, or with the investigation of the subject of taxation generally. Any corporation failing or refusing to obey any valid order or requirement of the commission, within such reasonable time, not less than ten days, as shall be fixed in the order, may be fined by the commission (proceeding by due process of law as aforesaid) such sum, not exceeding five hundred dollars, as the commission may deem proper, or such sum in excess of five hundred dollars, as may be prescribed, or authorized, by law; and each day's continuance of such failure or refusal, after due service upon such corporation of the older or requirement of the commission, shall be a separate offence provided that should the operation of such order or requirement be suspended pending an appeal therefrom, the period of such suspension shall not be computed against the company in the matter of its liability to fines or penalties

(d) From any action of the commission prescribing rates, charges or classifications of traffic, or affecting the train schedule of any transportation company, or requiring additional facilities, conveniences or public service of any transportation or transmission company, or refusing to approve a suspending bond, or requiring additional security thereon or an increase thereof, as provided for in sub-section e of this section, an appeal (subject to such reasonable limitations as to time, regulations as to procedure and provisions as to costs, as may be prescribed by law) may be taken by the corporation whose rates, charges or classifications of traffic, schedule, facilities, conveniences or service, are affected, or by any person deeming himself aggrieved by such action, or (if allowed by law) by the Commonwealth. Until otherwise provided by law, such appeal shall be taken in the manner in which appeals may be taken to the Supreme Court of Appeals from the inferior courts, except that such an appeal shall be of right, and the Supreme Court of Appeals may provide by rule for proceedings in the matter of appeals in any particular in which the existing rules of law are inapplicable. If such appeal be taken by the corporation whose rates, charges or classifications of traffic, schedules, facilities, conveniences or service are affected, the Commonwealth shall be made the appellee, but, in the other cases mentioned the corporation so affected shall be made the appellee. The General Assembly may also, by general laws, provide for appeals from any other action of the commission, by the Commonwealth or by any person interested, irrespective of the amount involved. All appeals from the commission shall be to the Supreme Court of Appeals only, aid in all appeals to which the Commonwealth is a party, it shall be represented by the Attorney General or his legally appointed representative. No court of this Commonwealth (except the Supreme Court of Appeals, by way of appeals as herein authorized) shall have jurisdiction to review, reverse, correct or annul any action of the commission, within the scope of its authority, or to suspend or delay the execution or operation thereof, or to enjoin, restrain or interfere with the commission in the performance of its official duties, provided, however, that the writs of mandamus and prohibition shall lie from the Supreme Court of Appeals to the commission in all cases where such writs, respectively, would lie to any inferior tribunal or officer.

(e) Upon the granting of an appeal, a writ of supersedeas may be awarded by the appellate court, suspending the operation of the action appealed from until the final disposition of the appeal, but, prior to the final reversal thereof by the appellate court, no action of the commission prescribing or affecting the rates, charges or classifications of traffic of any transportation or transmission company shall be delayed, or suspended, in its operation, by reason of any appeal by such corporation, or by reason of any proceedings resulting from such appeal, until a suspending bond shall first have been executed and filed with, and approved by, the commission (or approved on review by the Supreme Court of Appeals), payable to the Commonwealth, and sufficient in amount and security to insure the prompt refunding, by the appealing corporation to the parties entitled thereto of all charges which such company may collect or receive, pending the appeal, in excess of those fixed, or authorized, by the final decision of the court on appeal. The commission, upon the execution of such bond, shall forthwith require the appealing company, under penalty of the immediate enforcement (pending the appeal and notwithstanding any supersedeas), of the order or requirement appealed from, to keep such accounts, and to make to the commission, from time to time, such reports, verified by oath, as may, in the judgment of the commission, suffice to show the amounts being charged or received by the company pending the appeal, in excess of the charge allowed by the action of the commission appealed from, together with the names and addresses of the persons to whom such overcharges will be refundable in case the charges made by the company pending the appeal, be not sustained on such appeal, and the commission shall also, from time to time, require such company, under like penalty, to give additional security on, or to increase, the said suspending bond, whenever, in the opinion of the commission, the same may be necessary to insure the prompt refunding of the overcharges aforesaid. Upon the final decision of such appeal, all amounts which the appealing company may have collected, pending the appeal, in excess of that authorized by such final decision, shall be promptly refunded by the company to the parties entitled thereto, in such manner, and through such methods of distribution, as may be prescribed by the commission, or by law. All such appeals affecting rates, charges or classifications of traffic, shall have precedence upon the docket of the appellate court, and shall be heard and disposed of promptly by the court, irrespective of its place of session, next after the habeas corpus, and Commonwealth's cases already on the docket of the court.

(a) In no case of appeal from the commission shall any new or additional evidence be introduced in the appellate court, but the chairman of the commission, under the seal of the commission, shall certify to the appellate court all the facts upon which the action appealed from was based and which may be essential for the proper decision of the appeal, together with such of the evidence introduced before, or considered by, the commission as may be selected, specified and required to be certified, by any party in interest, as well as such other evidence, so introduced or considered, as the commission may deem proper to certify. The commission shall, whenever an appeal is taken therefrom, file with the record of the case, and as a part thereof, a written statement of the reasons upon which the action appealed from was based, and such statement shall be lead and considered by the appellate court, upon disposing of the appeal. The appellate court shall have jurisdiction, on such appeal, to consider and determine the reasonableness and justness of the action of the commission appealed from, as well as any other matter arising under such appeal provided, however, that the action of the commission appealed from shall be regarded as prima facie just, reasonable and correct, but the court may, when it deems necessary, in the interest of justice, demand to the commission any case pending on appeal, and require the same to be further investigated by the commission, and reported upon to the court (together with a certificate of such additional evidence as may be tendered before the commission by any party in interest), before the appeal is finally decided.

(b) Whenever the court, upon appeal, shall reverse an order of the commission affecting the rates, charges or the classification of traffic of any transportation or transmission company, it shall, at the same time, substitute therefor such order as in its opinion, the commission should have made at the time of entering the order appealed from, otherwise the reversal order shall not be valid. Such substituted order shall have the same force and effect (and none other) as if it had been entered by the commission at the time the original order appealed from was entered. The right of the commission to prescribe and enforce rates, charges, classifications, rules and regulations, affecting any or all actions of the commission theretofore entered by it and appealed from, but based upon circumstances or conditions different from those existing at the time the order appealed from was made, shall not be suspended or impaired by reason of the pendency of such appeal; but no order of the commission, prescribing or altering such rates, charges, classifications, rules or regulations, shall be retroactive.

(h) The right of any person to institute and prosecute in the ordinary courts of justice, any action, suit or motion against any transportation or transmission company, for any claim or cause of action against such company, shall not be extinguished or impaired, by reason of any fine or other penalty which the commission may impose, or be authorized to impose, upon such company because of its breach of any public duty, or because of its failure to comply with any order or requirement of the commission; but, in no such proceeding by any person against such corporation, nor in any collateral proceeding, shall the reasonableness, justness or validity of any rate, charge, classification or traffic, rule, regulation or requirement, theretofore prescribed by the commission, within the scope of its authority, and then in force, be questioned: provided, however, that no ease based upon or involving any order of the commission shall be heard, or disposed of, against the objection of either party, so long as such order is suspended in its operation by an order of the Supreme Court of Appeals as authorized by this Constitution or by any law passed in pursuance thereof.

(i) The commission shall make annual reports to the Governor of its proceedings, in which reports it shall recommend, from time to time, such new or additional legislation in reference to its powers or duties, or to the creation, supervision, regulation or control of corporations, or to the subject of taxation, as it may deem wise or expedient, or as may be required by law.

(k) Upon the organization of the State Corporation Commission, the Board of

Public Works and the office of Railroad Commissioner, shall cease to exist; and all books, papers and documents pertaining thereto, shall be transferred to, and become a part of the records of, the office of the State Corporation Commission.

(l) After the first day of January, nineteen hundred and five, in addition to the modes of amendment provided for in Article fifteen of this Constitution, the General Assembly, upon the recommendation of the State Corporation Commission, may, by law, from time to time, amend sub-sections a to i, inclusive, of this section, or any of them, or any such amendment thereof: provided, that no amendment made under authority of this sub-section shall contravene the provisions of any part of this Constitution other than the sub-sections last above referred to or any such amendment thereof.

SEC. 157. Provision shall be made by general laws for the payment of a fee to the Commonwealth by every domestic corporation, upon the granting, amendment or extension of its charter, and by every foreign corporation upon obtaining a license to do business in this State as specified in this section; and also for the payment, by every domestic corporation, and foreign corporation doing business in this State, of an annual registration fee of not less than five dollars nor more than twenty-five dollars, which shall be irrespective of any specific license, or other, tax imposed by law upon such company for the privilege of carrying on its business in this State, or upon its franchise or property; and for the making, by every such corporation (at the time of paying such annual registration fee), of such report to the State Corporation Commission, of the status, business or condition of such corporation, as the General Assembly may prescribe. No foreign corporation shall have authority to do business in this State, until it shall have first obtained from the commission a license to do business in this State, upon such terms and conditions as may be prescribed by law. The failure by any corporation for two successive years to pay its annual registration fee, or to make its said annual reports, shall, when such failure shall have continued for ninety days after the expiration of such two years, operate as a revocation and annulment of the charter of such corporation if it be a domestic company, or, of its license to do business in this State if it be a foreign company; and the General Assembly shall provide additional and suitable penalties for the failure of any corporation to comply promptly with the requirements of this section, or of any laws passed in pursuance thereof. The commission shall compel all corporations to comply promptly with such requirements, by enforcing, in the manner hereinbefore authorized, such fines and penalties against the delinquent company as may be provided for, or authorized by, this article; but the General Assembly may relieve from the payment of the said registration fee any purely charitable institution or institutions.

SEC. 158. Every corporation heretofore chartered in this State, which shall hereafter accept, or effect, any amendment or extension of its charter, shall be conclusively presumed to have thereby surrendered every exemption from taxation, and every non- repealable feature of its charter and of the amendments thereof, and also all exclusive rights or privileges theretofore granted to it by the General Assembly and not enjoyed by other corporations of a similar general character; and to have thereby agreed to thereafter hold its charter and franchises, and all amendments thereof, under the provisions and subject to all the requirements, terms and conditions of this Constitution and of any laws passed in pursuance thereof, so far as the same may be applicable to such corporation.

SEC. 159. The exercise of the right of eminent domain shall never be abridged, nor so construed as to prevent the General Assembly from taking the property and franchises of corporations and subjecting them to public use, the same as the property of individuals; and the exercise of the police power of the State shall never be abridged, nor so construed as to permit corporations to conduct their business in such manner as to infringe the equal rights of individuals or the general well-being of the State.

SEC. 160. No transportation or transmission company shall charge or receive any greater compensation, in the aggregate, for transporting the same class of passengers or property, or for transmitting the same class of messages, over a shorter than over a longer distance, along the same line and in the same direction-- the shorter being included in the longer distance, but this section shall not be construed as authoring any such company to charge or reserve as great compensation for a shorter as for a longer distance the State Corporation Commission may, from time to time, authorize any such company to disregard the foregoing provisions of this section, by charging such rates as the commission may prescribe as just and equitable between such company and the public, to or from any junctional or competitive points or localities, or where the competition of points located without this

State may make necessary the prescribing of special rates for the protection of the commerce of this State, but this section shall not apply to mileage tickets, or to any special excursion, or commutation, rates, or to special rates for services rendered to the government of this State, or of the United States, or in the interest of some public object, when such tickets or rates shall have been prescribed or authorized by the commission

SEC. 161. No transportation or transmission company doing business in this State shall grant to any member of the General Assembly, or to any state, county, district or municipal officer, except to members and officers of the State Corporation Commission for then personal use while in office, any frank, free pass, free transportation or any rebate or reduction in the rates charged by such company to the general public for like services. For violation of the provisions of this section the offending company shall be liable to such penalties as may be prescribed by law, and any member of the General Assembly, or any such officer, who shall, while in office, accept any gift, privilege or benefit as is prohibited by this section, shall thereby forfeit his office, and be subject to such further penalties as may be prescribed by law, but this section shall not prevent a street railway company from transporting free of charge any member of the police force or fire department while in the discharge of his official duties, nor prohibit the acceptance by any such policeman or fireman of such free transportation.

SEC 102. The doctrine of fellow servant, so far as it affects the liability of the master for injuries to his servant resulting from the acts or omissions of any other servant or servants of the common master, is, to the extent hereinafter stated, abolished as to every employee of a railroad company, engaged in the physical construction, repair or maintenance of its roadway, track or any of the structures connected therewith, or in any work in or upon a car or engine standing upon a track, or in the physical operation of a train, car, engine, or switch, or in any service requiring his presence upon a train, car or engine, and every such employee shall have the same right to recovery for every injury suffered by him from the acts or omissions of any other employee or employees of the common master, that a servant would have (at the time when this Constitution goes into effect), if such acts or omissions were those of the master himself in the performance of a non- assignable duty provided, that the injury, so suffered by such railroad employee, result from the negligence of an officer, or agent, of the company of a higher grade of service than himself, or from that of a person, employed by the company, having the right, or charged with the duty, to control or direct the general services or the immediate work of the party injured, or the general services or the immediate work of the co employee through, or by whose act or omission he is injured, or that it result from the negligence of a co employee engaged in another department of labor, or engaged upon, or in charge of, any car upon which, or upon the train of which it is a part, the injured employee is not at the time of receiving the injury, or who is in charge of any switch, signal point, or locomotive engine, or is charged with dispatching trains or transmitting telegraphic or telephonic orders therefore, and whether such negligence be in the performance of an assignable or non assignable duty. The physical construction, repair or maintenance of the roadway, track or any of the structures connected therewith, and the physical construction, repair, maintenance, cleaning or operation of trains, cars or engines, shall be regarded as different departments of labor within the meaning of this section. Knowledge, by any such railroad employee injured, of the defective or unsafe character or condition of any machinery, ways, appliances or structures, shall be no defence to an action for injury caused thereby. When death, whether instantaneous or not, results to such an employee from any injury for which he could have recovered, under the above provisions, had death not occurred, then his legal or personal representative, surviving consort, and relatives (and any trustee, curator committee or guardian of such consort or relatives) shall, respectively, have the same rights and remedies with respect thereto as if his death had been caused by the negligence of a co employee while in the performance, as vice-principal, of a non assignable duty of the master. Every contract or agreement, express or implied, made by an employee, to waive the benefit of this section, shall be null and void This section shall not be construed to deprive any employee, or his legal or personal representative, surviving consort or relatives (or any trustee, curator, committee or guardian of such consort or relatives), of an\ rights or remedies that he or they may have by the law of the land, at the time this Constitution goes into effect Nothing contained in this section shall restrict the power of the General Assembly to further enlarge, for the above named class of employees, the rights and remedies hereinbefore provided for, or to extend such rights and remedies to, or otherwise enlarge the present rights and remedies of, any other class of employees of railroads or of employees of any person, firm or corporation

SEC 163 No foreign corporation shall be authored to carry on, m this State, the business, or to exercise any of the powers or functions, of a public service corporation, or be permitted to do anything which domestic corporations are prohibited from doing or be relieved from compliance with any of the requirements made of similar domestic corporations by the Constitution and laws of this State, where the same can be made applicable to such foreign corporation without discriminating against it But this section shall not affect any public service corporation whose line or route extends across the boundary of this Commonwealth, nor prevent any foreign corporation from continuing in such lawful business as it may be actually engaged in within this State, when this Constitution goes into effect; but any such foreign public service corporation, so engaged, shall not, without first becoming incorporated under the laws of this State, be authorized to acquire, lease, use or operate, within this State, any public or municipal franchise or franchises in addition to such as it may own, lease, use or operate when this Constitution goes into effect. The property, within this State, of foreign corporations shall always be subject to attachment, the same as that of non- resident individuals; and nothing in this section shall restrict the power of the General Assembly to discriminate against foreign corporations whenever, and in whatsoever respect, it may deem wise or expedient.

SEC. 164. The right of the Commonwealth, through such instrumentalities as it may select, to prescribe and define the public duties of all common carriers and public service corporations, to regulate and control them in the performance of their public duties, and to fix and limit their charges therefor, shall never be surrendered nor abridged.

SEC. 165. The General Assembly shall enact laws preventing all trusts, combinations and monopolies, inimical to the public welfare.

SEC. 166. The exclusive right to build or operate railroads parallel to its own, or any other, line of railroad, shall not be granted to any company; but every railroad company shall have the right, subject to such reasonable regulations as may be prescribed by law, to parallel, intersect, connect with or cross, with its roadway, any other railroad or railroads; but no railroad company shall build or operate any line of railroad not specified in its charter, or in some amendment thereof. All railroad companies, whose lines of railroad connect, shall receive and transport each other's passengers, freight, loaded or empty cars, without delay or discrimination. Nothing in this section shall deprive the General Assembly of the right to prevent by statute, repealable at pleasure, any railroad from being built parallel to the present line of the Richmond, Fredericksburg and Potomac railroad.

SEC. 167. The General Assembly shall enact general laws regulating and controlling all issues of stock and bonds by corporations. Whenever stock or bonds are to be issued by a corporation, it shall, before issuing the same, file with the State Corporation Commission a statement (verified by the oath of the president or secretary of the corporation, and in such form as may be prescribed or permitted by the commission) setting forth fully and accurately the basis, or financial plan, upon which such stock or bonds are to be issued; and where such basis or plan includes services or property (other than money), received or to be received by the company, such statement shall accurately specify and describe, in the manner prescribed, or permitted, by the commission, the services and property, together with the valuation at which the same are received or to be received; and such corporation shall comply with any other requirements or restrictions which may be imposed by law. The General Assembly shall provide adequate penalties for the violation of this section, or of any laws passed in pursuance thereof; and it shall be the duty of the commission to adjudge, and enforce (in the manner hereinbefore provided), against any corporation refusing or failing to comply with the provisions of this section, or of any laws passed in prey nuance thereof, such fines and penalties as are authorized by this Constitution, or may be prescribed by law.

ARTICLE XIII.
TAXATION AND FINANCE.

SEC. 168. All property, except as hereinafter provided, shall be taxed; all taxes, whether state, local, or municipal, shall be uniform upon the same class of subjects within the territorial limits of the authority levying the tax, and shall be levied and collected under general laws.

SEC. 169. Except as hereinafter provided, all assessments of real estate and tangible personal property shall be at their fair market value, to be ascertained as prescribed by law. The General Assembly may allow a lower rate of taxation to be imposed for a period of years by a city or town upon land added to its corporate limits, than is imposed on similar property within its limits at the time such land is added. Nothing in this Constitution shall prevent the General Assembly, after the first day of January, nineteen hundred and thirteen, from segregating for the purposes of taxation, the several kinds or classes of property, so as to specify and determine upon what subjects, state taxes, and upon what subjects, local taxes may be levied.

SEC. 170. The General Assembly may levy a tax on incomes in excess of six hundred dollars per annum; may levy a license tax upon any business which cannot be reached by the ad valorem system; and may impose state franchise taxes, and in imposing a franchise tax, may, in its discretion, make the same in lieu of taxes upon other property, in whole or in part, of a transportation, industrial, or commercial corporation. Whenever a franchise tax shall be imposed upon a corporation doing business in this State, or whenever all the capital, however invested, of a corporation chartered under the laws of this State, shall be taxed, the shares of stock issued by any such corporation, shall not be further taxed. No city or town shall impose any tax or assessment upon abutting land owners for street or other public local improvements, except for making and improving the walkways upon then existing streets, and improving and paving then existing alleys, and for either the construction, or for the use of sewers; and the same when imposed, shall not be in excess of the peculiar benefits resulting therefrom to such abutting land owners. Except in cities and towns, no such taxes or assessments, for local public improvements shall be imposed on abutting land owners.

SEC. 171. The General Assembly shall provide for a re-assessment of real estate, in the year nineteen, hundred and five, and every fifth year thereafter, except that of railway and canal corporations, which, after the January the first, nineteen hundred and thirteen, may be assessed as the General Assembly may provide

SEC 172 The General Assembly shall provide for the special and separate assessment of all coal and other mineral land, but until such special assessment is made, such land shall be assessed under existing laws

SEC 173 The General Assembly shall levy a state capitation tax of, and not exceeding, one dollar and fifty cents per annum on every male resident of the State not less than twenty one years of age, except those pensioned by this State for military services, one dollar of which shall be applied exclusively in aid of the public free schools, in proportion to the school population, and the residue shall be returned and paid by the State into the treasury of the county or city in which it was collected, to be appropriated by the proper county or city authorities to such county or city purposes as they shall respectively determine, but said state capitation tax shall not be a lien upon, nor collected by legal process from, the personal property which may be exempt from levy or distress under the poor debtor's law. The General Assembly may authorize the board of supervisors of any county, or the council of any city or town, to levy an additional capitation tax not exceeding one dollar per annum on every such resident within its limits, which shall be applied in aid of the public schools of such county, city or town, or for such other county, city or town purposes as they shall determine

SEC 174 After this Constitution shall be in force, no statute of limitation shall run against any claim of the State for taxes upon any property, nor shall the failure to assess property for taxation defeat a subsequent assessment for and collection of taxes for any preceding year or years, unless such property shall have passed to a bona fide purchaser of value, without notice, in which latter case the property shall be assessed for taxation against such purchaser from the date of his purchase

SEC 175 The natural oyster beds, rocks and shoals, in the waters of this State, shall not be leased, rented or sold, but shall be held in trust for the benefit of the people of this State, subject to such regulations and restrictions as the General Assembly may prescribe, but the General Assembly may, from time to time, define and determine such natural beds, rocks or shoals, by surveys or otherwise

SEC 176 The State Corporation Commission shall annually ascertain and assess, at the time hereinafter mentioned, and in the manner required of the Board of Public Works, by the law in force on January the first nineteen hundred and two, the value of the roadbed, and other real estate, rolling stock, and all other personal property whatsoever (except its franchise and the non taxable shares of stock issued by other corporations) in this State, of each railway corporation, whatever its motive power, now or hereafter liable for taxation upon such property, the canal bed and other real estate, the boats and all other personal property whatsoever (except its franchise and the non taxable shares of stock issued by other corporations) in this State, of each canal corporation, empowered to conduct transportation, and such property shall be taxed for state, county, city, town and district purposes in the same manner as authorized by said law, at such rates of taxation as may be imposed by them, respectively, from time to time, upon the real estate and personal property of natural persons provided, that no tax shall be laid upon the net income of such corporations.

SEC. 177. Each such railway or canal corporation, including also any such as is exempt from taxation as to its works, visible property, or profits, shall also pay an annual state franchise tax equal to one per centum upon the gross receipts hereinafter specified in section One Hundred and Seventy eight for the privilege of exercising its franchise in this State, which, with the taxes provided for in section One Hundred and Seventy six, shall be in lieu of all other taxes or license charges whatsoever upon the franchises of such corporation, the shares of stock issued by it, and upon its property assessed under section One Hundred and Seventy six provided, that nothing herein contained shall exempt such corporation from the annual fee required by section One Hundred and fifty seven of this Constitution, or from assessments for street and other public local improvements authorized by section One Hundred and Seventy, and provided, further, that nothing herein contained shall annul or interfere with, or prevent any contract or agreement by ordinance between street railway corporations and municipalities, as to compensation for the use of the streets or alleys of such municipalities by such railway corporations.

SEC 178 The amount of such franchise tax shall be equal to one per centum of the gross transportation receipts of such corporation, for the year ending June the thirtieth of each year, to be ascertained by the State Corporation Commission, in the following manner:

(a) When the road or canal of the corporation lies wholly within this State, the tax shall be equal to one per centum of the entire gross transportation receipts of such corporation

(b) When the road or canal of the corporation lies partly within and partly without this State or is operated as a part of a line or system extending beyond this State, the tax shall be equal to one per centum of the gross transportation receipts earned within this State, to be determined as follows: By ascertaining the average gross transportation receipts per mile over its whole extent within and without this State, and multiplying the result by the number of miles operated within this State provided, that from the sum so ascertained there may be a reasonable deduction because of any excess of value of the terminal facilities or other similar advantages in other states over similar facilities or advantages in this State.

SEC 179 Each corporation mentioned in sections One Hundred and Seventy six and One Hundred and Seventy seven shall annually, on the first day of September, make to the State Corporation Commission the report which the law, in force January the first, nineteen hundred and two, required to be made annually to the Board of Public Works by every railroad and canal company in this State, not exempt from taxation by virtue of its charter, which report shall also show the property taxable in this State belonging to the corporation on the thirtieth day of June preceding, and its total gross transportation receipts for the year ending on that date. Upon receiving such report the State Corporation Commission shall, after thirty days' notice previously given, as provided by said law, assess the value of the property not exempt from taxation, of the corporation, and ascertain the amount of the franchise tax and other state taxes chargeable against it. All taxes for which the corporation is liable shall be paid on or before the first day of December following the provisions of said law, except as changed by this article shall apply to the ascertainment and collection of the franchise, as well as other taxes of such corporations. Said taxes, until paid, shall be a lien upon the property within this State of the corporation owning the same, and take precedence of all other liens or incumbrances.

SEC. 180 Any corporation aggrieved by the assessment and ascertainment made under sections One Hundred and Seventy six and One Hundred and Seventy eight may, within thirty days after receiving a certified copy thereof, apply for relief to the circuit court of the city of Richmond Justice of the application, setting forth the grounds of complaint, verified by affidavit, shall be served on the State Corporation Commission, and on the Attorney General whose duty it shall be to represent the State. The court, if of opinion that the assessment or tax is excessive shall reduce the same, but if of opinion that it is insufficient, shall increase the same. Unless the applicant paid the taxes under protest, when due, the court, if it disallow the application, shall give judgment against it for a sum, by way of damages, equal to interest at the rate of one per centum per month upon the amount of taxes from the time the same were payable. If the application be allowed, in whole or in part, appropriate relief shall be granted, including the right to recover any excess of taxes that may have been paid, with legal interest thereon, and costs, from the State or local authorities, or both, as the case may be, the judgment to be enforceable by mandamus or other proper process issuing from the court finally adjudicating the application. Subject to the provisions of Article Six of this Constitution, the Supreme Court of Appeals may allow a court of error to either party.

SEC. 181. As of January the first, nineteen hundred and three, the system of taxation, as to the corporations mentioned in sections One Hundred and Seventy six and One Hundred and Seventy seven, shall be as set forth in sections One Hundred and Seventy six to One Hundred and Eighty, inclusive, and for that year the franchise tax shall be based upon such gross receipts for the year ending the thirtieth day of June, nineteen hundred and three, and such system shall so remain until the first day of January, nineteen hundred and thirteen, and thereafter until modified or changed, as may be prescribed by law provided, that, if the said system shall for any reason become inoperative, the General Assembly shall have power to adopt some other system.

SEC. 182. Until otherwise prescribed by law, the shares of stock issued by trust or security companies chartered by this State, and by incorporated banks, shall be taxed in the same manner in which the shares of stock issued by incorporated banks were taxed, by the law in force January the first, nineteen hundred and two, but from the total assessed value of the shares of stock of any such company or bank, there shall be deducted the assessed value of its real estate otherwise taxed in this State, and the value of each share of stock shall be its proportion of the remainder.

SEC. 183. Except as otherwise provided in this Constitution, the following property and no other, shall be exempt from taxation, state and local, but the General Assembly may hereafter tax any of the property hereby exempted save that mentioned in sub-section (a)

(a) Property directly or indirectly owned by the State, however held, and property lawfully owned and held by counties, cities, towns, or school districts, used wholly and exclusively for county, city, town, or public school purposes, and obligations issued by the State since the fourteenth day of February, eighteen hundred and eighty two or hereafter exempted by law. (b) Buildings with land they actually occupy, and the furniture and furnishings therein lawfully owned and held by churches or religious bodies, and wholly and exclusively used for religious worship, or for the residence of the minister of any such church or religious body, together with the additional adjacent land reasonably necessary for the convenient use of any such building.

(c) Private family burying grounds not exceeding one acre in area, reserved as such by will or deed or shown by other sufficient evidence to be reserved as such, and so exclusively used, and public burying grounds and lots therein exclusively used for burial purposes, and not conducted for profit, whether owned or managed by local authorities or by private corporations.

(d) Buildings with the land they actually occupy and the furniture, furnishings, books and instruments therein, wholly devoted to educational purposes, belonging to, and actually and exclusively occupied and used by churches, public libraries, incorporated colleges, academies, industrial schools, seminaries, or other incorporated institutions of learning, including the Virginia Historical Society, which are not corporations having shares of stock or otherwise owned by individuals or other corporations, together with such additional adjacent land owned by such churches, libraries and educational institutions as may be reasonably necessary for the convenient use of such buildings, respectively, and also the buildings thereon used as residences by the officers or instructors of such educational institutions, and also the permanent endowment funds held by such libraries and educational institutions directly or in trust, and not invested in real estate provided, that such libraries and educational institutions are not conducted for profit of any person or persons, natural or corporate directly or under any guise or pretence whatsoever. But the exemption mentioned in this sub section shall not apply to any industrial school, individual or corporate, not the property of the State, which does work for compensation, or manufactures and sells articles, in the community in which such school is located; provided, that nothing herein contained shall restrict any such school from doing work for or selling its own products or any other articles to any of its students or employees.

(e) Real estate belonging to, actually and exclusively occupied, and used by, and personal property, including endowment funds, belonging to Young Men's Christian Associations, and other similar religious associations, orphan or other asylums, reformatories, hospitals and nunneries, which are not conducted for profit, but purely and completely as charities.

(f) Buildings with the land they actually occupy, and the furniture and furnishings therein, belonging to any benevolent or charitable association and used exclusively for lodge purposes or meeting rooms by such association, together with such additional adjacent land as may be necessary for the convenient rise of the buildings for such purposes; and

(g) Property belonging to the Association for the Preservation of Virginia Antiquities, the Confederate Memorial Literary Society, and the Mount Vernon Ladies' Association of the Union.

No inheritance tax shall be charged, directly or indirectly, against any legacy or devise made according to law for the benefit of any institution or other body or any natural or corporate person whose property is exempt from taxation as hereinbefore mentioned in this section.

Nothing contained in this section shall be construed to exempt from taxation the property of any person, firm, association or corporation, who shall, expressly or impliedly, directly or indirectly, contract or promise to pay any sum of money or other benefit, on account of death, sickness, or accident to any of its members or any other person; and whenever any building or land, or part thereof, mentioned in this section and not belonging to the State, shall be leased or shall be a source of revenue or profit, all of such buildings and land shall be liable to taxation as other land and buildings in the same county, city, or town; and nothing herein contained shall be construed as authorizing or requiring any county, city, or town to tax for county, city or town purposes, in violation of the rights of the lessees thereof existing under any lawful contract heretofore made, any real estate owned by such county, city or town, and heretofore leased by it.

Obligations issued by counties, cities, or towns may be exempted by the authorities of such localities from local taxation.

SEC. 184. No debt shall be contracted by the State except to meet casual deficits in the revenue, to redeem a previous liability of the State, to suppress insurrection, repel invasion, or defend the State in time of war. No scrip, certificate, or other evidence of state indebtedness, shall be issued except for the transfer or redemption of stock previously issued, or for such debts as are expressly authorized in this Constitution.

SEC. 185. Neither the credit of the State, nor of any county, city, or town, shall be, directly or indirectly, under any device or pretence whatsoever, granted to or in aid of any person, association, or corporation; nor shall the State, or any county, city, or town subscribe to or become interested in the stock or obligations of any company, association, or corporation, for the purpose of aiding in the construction or maintenance of its work; nor shall the State become a party to or become interested in any work of internal improvement, except public roads, or engaged in carrying on any such work; nor assume any indebtedness of any county, city, or town, nor lend its credit to the same; but this section shall not prevent a county, city or town from perfecting a subscription to the capital stock of a railroad company authorized by existing charter conditioned upon the affirmative vote of the voters and freeholders of such county, city or town in favor of such subscription: provided, that such vote be had prior to July first, nineteen hundred and three.

SEC. 186. All taxes, licenses, and other revenue of the State, shall be collected by its proper officers and paid into the state treasury. No money shall be paid out of the state treasury except in pursuance of appropriations made by law; and no such appropriation shall be made which is payable more than two years after the end of the session of the General Assembly, at which the law is enacted authorizing the same; and no appropriation shall be made for the payment of any debt or obligation created in the name of the State during the war between the Confederate States and the United States. Nor shall any county, city, or town pay any debt or obligation created by such county, city, or town in aid of said war.

SEC. 187. The General Assembly shall provide and maintain a sinking fund in accordance with the provisions of section Ten of the act, approved February the twentieth, eighteen hundred and ninety-two, entitled "an act to provide for the settlement of the public debt of Virginia not funded under the provisions of an act entitled an act to ascertain and declare Virginia's equitable share of the debt created before, and actually existing at the time of the partition of her territory and resources, and to provide for the issuance of bonds covering the same, and the regular and prompt payment of the interest theron, approved February the fourteenth, eighteen hundred and eighty-two." Every law hereafter enacted by the General Assembly, creating a debt or authorizing a loan, shall provide for the creation and maintenance of a sinking fund for the payment or redemption of the same.

SEC. 188. No other or greater amount of tax or revenue shall, at any time, be levied than may be required for the necessary expenses of the government, or to pay the indebtedness of the State.

SEC. 189. On all lands and the improvements thereon, and on all tangible personal property, not exempt from taxation by the provision of this article, the rate of state taxation shall be twenty cents on every hundred dollars of the assessed value thereof, the proceeds of which shall be applied to the expenses of the government and the indebtedness of the State, and a further tax of ten cents on every hundred dollars of the assessed value thereof, which shall be applied to the support of the public free schools of the State: provided, that after the first day of January, nineteen hundred and seven, the tax rate upon said real and personal property, for such purposes shall be prescribed by law. But the General Assembly during such period of four years, in addition to making annually an appropriation for pensions not to exceed the last appropriation made for such purpose prior to September the thirtieth, nineteen hundred and one, may levy annually, a special tax for pensions, on such real and personal property of not exceeding five cents on the hundred dollars of the assessed value therof.

ARTICLE XIV.
MISCELLANEOUS PROVISIONS.
HOMESTEAD AND OTHER EXEMPTIONS.

SEC. 190. Every householder or head of a family shall be entitled, in addition to the articles now exempt from levy or distress for rent, to hold exempt from levy, seizure, garnishment, or sale under any execution, order, or other process issued on any demand for a debt hereafter contracted, his real and personal property, or either, including money and debts due him, to the value of not exceeding two thousand dollars, to be selected by him: provided, that such exemption shall not extend to any execution, order, or other process issued on any demand in the following cases:

First. For the purchase price of said property, or any part thereof. If the property purchased, and not paid for, be exchanged for, or converted into, other property by the debtor, such last- named property shall not be exempted from the payment of such unpaid purchase money under the provisions of this article;

Second. For services rendered by a laboring person or mechanic;

Third. For liabilities incurred by any public officer, or officer of a court, or any fiduciary, or any attorney-at-law for money collected;

Fourth. For a lawful claim for any taxes, levies, or assessments accruing after the first day of June, eighteen hundred and sixty- six;

Fifth. For rent;

Sixth. For the legal or taxable fees of any public officer or officer of a court.

SEC. 191. The said exemption shall not be claimed or held in a shifting stock of merchandise, or in any property, the conveyance of which by the homestead claimant has been set aside on the ground of fraud or want of consideration.

SEC. 192. The General Assembly shall prescribe the manner and the conditions on which a householder or head of a family shall set apart and hold for himself and family a homestead in any of the property hereinbefore mentioned. But this section shall not be construed as authorizing the General Assembly to defeat or impair the benefits intended to be conferred by the provisions of this article.

SEC. 193. Nothing contained in this article shall invalidate any homestead exemption heretofore claimed under the provisions of the former Constitution; or impair in any manner the right of any householder or head of a family existing at the time that this Constitution goes into effect, to select the exemption, or any part thereof, to which he was entitled under the former Constitution; provided that such right, if hereafter exercised, be not in conflict with the exemptions set forth in sections One Hundred and Ninety and One Hundred and Ninety-one. But no person who has selected and received the full exemption allowed by the former Constitution shall be entitled to select an additional exemption under this Constitution; and no person who has selected and received part of the exemption allowed by the former Constitution shall be entitled to select an additional exemption beyond the difference between the value of such part and a total valuation of two thousand dollars. So far as necessary to accomplish the purposes of this section the provisions of chapter One Hundred and Seventy-eight of the Code of Virginia, and the acts amendatory thereof, shall remain in force until repealed by the General Assembly. The provisions of this article shall be liberally construed.

SEC. 194. The General Assembly is hereby prohibited from passing any law staying the collection of debts, commonly known as "stay laws"; but this section shall not be construed as prohibiting any legislation which the General Assembly may deem necessary to fully carry out the provisions of this article.

HEIRS OF PROPERTY.

SEC. 195. The children of parents, one or both of whom were slaves at and during the period of cohabitation, and who were recognized by the father as his children, and whose mother was recognized by such father as his wife, and was cohabited with as such, shall be as capable of inheriting any estate whereof such father may have died seized, or possessed, or to which he was entitled, as though they had been born in lawful wedlock.

ARTICLE XV.
FUTURE CHANGES IN THE CONSTITUTION.

SEC. 196. Any amendment or amendments to the Constitution may be proposed in the Senate or House of Delegates, and if the same shall be agreed it by a majority of the members elected to each of the two houses, such proposed amendment or amendments shall be entered on their journals, with the ayes and noes taken thereon, and referred to the General Assembly at its first regular session held after the next general election of members of the House of Delegates, and shall be published for three months previous to the time of such election. If, at such regular session the proposed amendment or amendments shall be agreed to by a majority of all the members elected to each house, then it shall be the duty of the General Assembly to submit such proposed amendment or amendments to the people, in such manner and at such times as it shall prescribe; and if the people shall approve and ratify such amendment or amendments by a majority of the electors, qualified to vote for members of the General Assembly, noting thereon, such Amendment or amendments shall become part of the Constitution.

SEC. 197. At such time as the General Assembly may provide, a majority of the members elected to each house being recorded in the affirmative, the question, "shall there be a convention to revise the Constitution and amend the same?" shall be submitted to the electors qualified to vote for members of the General Assembly; and in case a majority of the electors so qualified, voting thereon, shall vote in favor of a convention for such purpose, the General Assembly, at its next session, shall provide for the election of delegates to such convention; and no convention for such purpose shall be otherwise called.

SCHEDULE.

That no inconvenience may arise from the adoption of this Constitution, and in order to provide for carrying it into complete operation, it is hereby ordained that:

SECTION 1. The common law and the statute laws in force at the time this Constitution goes into effect, so far as not repugnant thereto or repealed thereby, shall remain in force until they expire by their own limitation, or are altered or repealed by the General Assembly.

SEC. 2. All ordinances adopted by this Contention and appended to the official original draft of the Constitution delivered to the Secretary of the Commonwealth shall have the same force and effect, as if they were parts of this Constitution.

SEC. 3. Except as modified by this Constitution, all writs, actions and causes of action, prosecutions, lights of individuals, of bodies corporate or politic, and of the State, shall continue. All legal proceedings, civil and criminal, pending at the time this Constitution goes into effect, or instituted prior to the first day of February, nineteen hundred and four, in any county or circuit court as now existing, shall be prosecuted therein: provided, that all such matters, which are not finally terminated before the day last above mentioned, shall, on that date, by operation of this Constitution and Schedule, be transferred to the circuit court of the county or city created under this Constitution, and shall be proceeded with therein. All such matters pending in the city courts, preserved by this Constitution, when the same goes into effect, or thereafter instituted therein, shall continue in said courts, and be therein proceeded with, until otherwise provided by law. All matters before justices of the peace or police justices at the time this Constitution goes into effect, shall be proceeded with before them, until otherwise provided by law. All legal proceedings prosecuted after this Constitution goes into effect, whether in any of the courts now existing, or in those created by this Constitution, shall be proceeded with in the manner now or hereafter provided by law, except as otherwise required by this Constitution.

SEC. 4. All taxes, fines, penalties, forfeitures and escheats, accrued or accruing to the Commonwealth, or to any political subdivision thereof, under the present Constitution, or under the laws now in force, shall, under this Constitution, enure to the use of the Commonwealth, or of such subdivision thereof

SEC 5 All recognizances, and other obligations, and all other instruments entered into or executed before the adoption of this Constitution, or before the complete organization of the departments thereunder, to the Commonwealth, or to any county, or political subdivision thereof, city, town board, or other public corporation, or institution therein, or to any public officer, shall remain binding and valid, and rights and liabilities thereunder shall continue and may be enforced or prosecuted in the courts of this State as now or here after provided by law

SEC 6 From the day this Constitution goes into effect, the present judges of the Supreme Court of Appeals, or their successors then in office, shall be the judges of the Supreme Court of Appeals created by this Constitution, and continue in office, unless sooner removed, until February the first, nineteen hundred and seven. The jurisdiction of the court shall be as now or hereafter provided by law, subject to the provisions of this Constitution. All proceedings, then pending in the court as now organized, shall, by virtue of this Constitution, be transferred to and disposed of by the court created by this Constitution.

SEC 7 The present judicial system of county and circuit courts of the Commonwealth is continued, and the terms of the several judges thereof, with the powers and duties now possessed by them respectively, are continued, until the first day of February, nineteen hundred and four, as if this Constitution had not been adopted, on which day the judicial system of circuit courts created by this Constitution shall go into operation. The terms of the judges of the city courts, as preserved by this Constitution, of the cities of Alexandria, Charlottesville, Danville, Fredericksburg, Lynchburg, Petersburg, Norfolk, Portsmouth, Richmond, Staunton, Manchester, Roanoke, Winchester, and Newport News, shall continue until the first day of February, nineteen hundred and seven, and the terms of the judges of the city courts, as preserved by this Constitution, of the cities of Bristol, Radford and Buena Vista, shall continue until the first day of February, nineteen hundred and four, unless the said courts shall be sooner abolished The privilege now allowed by statute to judges of county courts and to judges of certain city courts to practice law, shall continue during the terms of the judges whose terms are continued by the Schedule, unless otherwise provided by-law

SEC 8 The terms of the clerks of the county and circuit courts now in office, or their successors, shall continue until the first day of February, nineteen hundred and four, and thereupon, the several clerks of the county courts in those counties in which such clerks are now ex-officio clerks of the circuit courts of said counties shall be and become the county clerks of their respective counties, and the clerks of all the other county courts of the State, except the counties of Accomac, Augusta, Bedford, Campbell, Elizabeth City, Fairfax, Lee, Loudoun Hanover Henrico, Rockingham, Nansemond, Southampton, Pittsylvania, Nelson and Fauquier, and, as such, the clerks of the circuit courts created therefor by this Constitution, and shall hold office as such until the first day of January, nineteen hundred and six, unless sooner removed, and then successors shall be elected on Tuesday after the first Monday in November, nineteen hundred and five, provided that the first term of the clerks so elected be for six years. In the counties of Accomac, Augusta, Bedford, Campbell, Elizabeth City, Fairfax, Lee, Loudoun, Hanover, Henrico, Rockingham, Nansemond, Southampton, Pittsylvania, Nelson and Fauquier, in which there are now separate clerks for the county and circuit courts thereof, there shall be elected on Tuesday after the first Monday in November nineteen hundred and three, county clerks for such counties. The terms of the clerks now in office, or their successors, of the several city courts preserved by this Constitution, shall continue until the first day of January, nineteen hundred and seven, and their successors shall be elected on Tuesday after the first Monday in November, nineteen hundred and five, but if any of such city courts shall be sooner abolished as provided in this Constitution or by law, then the term of the clerk of any such court shall thereupon determine.

SEC 9 The first election of the Governor and of all officers required by this Constitution, to be chosen by the qualified voters of the State at large, shall be held on the Tuesday after the first Monday in November, nineteen hundred and five, and their terms of office shall begin on the first day of February following their election. The present incumbents of said offices, or their successors, shall continue in office until the last named day.

SEC 10 The first election of members of the House of Delegates, and of all county and district officers, to be elected by the people under this Constitution, except as otherwise provided in this Schedule, shall be held on Tuesday after the first Monday in November, in the year nineteen hundred and three, and the terms of office of the several officers elected at that or any subsequent election shall begin on the first day of January, next after their election, except as otherwise provided in this Constitution or in this Schedule. And the terms of the office of the sheriff, commonwealth's attorney, treasurer, commissioners of the revenue, superintendents of the poor, supervisors of the several counties, justices of the peace, and overseers of the poor, and of any incumbent of any other county or district office not abolished by this Constitution, nor herein specifically mentioned, now in office, or their successors, or whose terms of office shall begin on the first day of July, nineteen hundred and two, are continued until January the first, nineteen hundred and four.

The terms of the present members of the House of Delegates, and the terms of the senators now in office, or (in case of vacancies therein), their successors, representing the senatorial districts bearing even numbers, are extended until the second Wednesday in January, nineteen hundred and four, provided, that the term of the senator, now residing m the city of Richmond, who by the provisions of the apportionment act, approved April the second, nineteen hundred and two, is continued in office as one of the senators from the thirty-eighth senatorial district thereby created, be extended until the second Wednesday in January, nineteen hundred and six. The terms of the senators now in office, or (in case of vacancies therein), their successors, representing the senatorial districts bearing odd numbers are extended until the second Wednesday in January, nineteen hundred and six.

In the senatorial districts bearing even numbers, there shall be elected, on the Tuesday after the first Monday in November, nineteen hundred and three, for a term of four years, to begin on the second Wednesday in January succeeding their election, members of the Senate to represent such districts; in the senatorial districts bearing odd numbers, and in the city of Richmond to fill the vacancy, which will, as above provided, occur on the second Wednesday in January, nineteen hundred and six, there shall be elected, on the Tuesday after the first Monday in November, nineteen hundred and five, for a term of two years, to begin on the second Wednesday in January succeeding their election, members of the Senate to represent such districts; and on the Tuesday after the first Monday in November, nineteen hundred and seven, there shall be elected, for the term of four years, to begin on the second Wednesday in January succeeding their election, a senator from each senatorial district in the State.

SEC. 11. All other state, county, and district officers, and their successors, who may be in office at the time this Constitution goes into effect, except the Auditor of Public Accounts, the Second Auditor, the Register of the Land Office, the Superintendent of Public Printing, the Commissioner of Labor and Industrial Statistics, Railroad Commissioner, notaries public, the Adjutant-General, the Superintendent and the Surgeon of the Penitentiary, the Manager and the Surgeon of the State Prison Farm, the superintendents of the several state hospitals, and the school superintendents for counties and cities, and school trustees, shall, unless their respective offices be abolished, or unless otherwise provided by this Constitution or Schedule, hold their respective offices, and discharge the respective duties and exercise the respective powers thereof, until January the first, nineteen hundred and four. The terms of the present incumbents in the offices of Auditor of Public Accounts, Second Auditor, Register of the Land Office, Superintendent of Public Printing, and Commissioner of Labor and Industrial Statistics, shall continue until March the first, nineteen hundred and four. The term of the Railroad Commissioner shall end as soon as the State Corporation Commission shall be organized. Notaries public shall continue in office until their respective commissions shall expire. The term of the office of Adjutant-General shall expire March the first, nineteen hundred and six. The Superintendent and the Surgeon of the Penitentiary, the Manager and the Surgeon of the State Prison Farm, the superintendents of the several state hospitals, shall continue in office until their successors shall be appointed by the respective boards empowered under this Constitution to make the several appointments. The school superintendents for counties and cities shall remain in office for their respective terms, and until their successors are appointed. School trustees now in office, or their successors, shall remain in office until otherwise provided by law. Electoral boards with the powers conferred by existing laws, except the appointment of registrars, shall remain in office until March, the first, nineteen hundred and four.

SEC. 12. The terms of the State Board of Education, the State Corporation Commission, and the Board of Agriculture and Immigration, the directors of public institutions and prisons, and of each state hospital, and the Commissioner of State Hospitals, to be first elected, or appointed, under this Constitution, shall begin on March the first, nineteen hundred and three. The board of any of the above-named departments and institutions as now constituted shall continue until the boards created under this Constitution for such departments and institutions respectively are duly organized. And the terms of the members of the Board of Fisheries are continued until March the first, nineteen hundred and six. The terms of the trustees or visitors of the state educational institutions, and other honorary appointments made by the Governor, are continued until otherwise provided by law.

SEC. 13. Charters of incorporation may, until the first day of April, nineteen hundred and three, be granted or amended by the courts of the State in accordance with the laws in force when this Constitution goes into effect, unless the General Assembly shall sooner provide for the creation of corporations as required by this Constitution.

SEC. 14. The terms of all officers elected by the qualified voters of a city, and of their successors, in office at the time this Constitution goes into effect, or whose terms of office begin on the first day of July, nineteen hundred and two, except the terms of mayors, of members of city councils and of the clerks of city courts, are continued until January the first, nineteen hundred and six; and their successors shall be elected on the Tuesday after the first Monday in November, nineteen hundred and five. The terms of all city officers, not so elected, shall expire as provided in the charters of the several cities, or as may be provided by law.

SEC. 15. Until otherwise provided by law, the mayors of the several cities shall continue in office until September the first, nineteen hundred and four, and their successors shall be elected the second Tuesday in June, nineteen hundred and four. Until otherwise provided by law, the members of the several city councils shall continue in office for the terms prescribed in the charters of their respective cities, except that where their terms are prescribed as ending on the first day of July of any year, they shall be extended until the first day of September following.

SEC. 16. Vacancies in any office, the term of which is confirmed or extended by this Schedule, occurring during such term or extension thereof, shall be filled in the manner prescribed by law.

Sec. 17. All officers, whose terms of office are extended by this Schedule, required by law or municipal ordinance to give bond for the faithful discharge of the duties of their respective offices, shall, prior to the expiration of the terms for which they were respectively chosen, before the court or other authority before whom such officer was required by law or municipal ordinance to give such bond, enter into a new bond, in the same penalty and with such security as was prescribed by law or municipal ordinance in respect to his former bond, and with like conditions as therein prescribed, for the faithful discharge of the duties of his office for the extended term herein provided for, and until his successor shall have been duly chosen, and shall have qualified according to law. Upon failure to give such bond within the time above prescribed, the office shall, upon the expiration of the term for which the incumbent thereof was chosen, become vacant,

SEC. 18. In all elections held after this Constitution goes into effect, the qualifications of electors shall be those required by Article Two of this Constitution.

SEC. 19. The General Assembly which convened on the first Wednesday in December, nineteen hundred and one, shall be called by the Governor to meet in session at the Capitol at twelve o'clock P.M., on Tuesday, the fifteenth day of July, nineteen hundred and two. It shall be vested with all the powers, charged with all the duties, and subject to all the limitations prescribed by this Constitution in reference to the General Assembly, except as to the limitation upon the period of its session, qualifications of members, and as to the time at which any of its acts shall take effect; but the ineligibility of the members thereof to be elected to any other office during their terms as members of the General Assembly shall be such as is imposed by this Constitution. The said General Assembly shall elect judges for all of the circuit courts provided for in this Constitution, and also of the corporation courts for Bristol, Radford, and Buena Vista, unless said city courts are sooner abolished.

SEC. 20. The said General Assembly shall enact such laws as may be deemed proper, including those necessary to put this Constitution into complete operation; to confirm those officers whose appointment is made by this Constitution subject to confirmation by the General Assembly or either house thereof; and to transact other proper business; and such session shall continue so long as may be necessary. The members shall receive for their services four dollars per day, for the time when the General Assembly is actually in session, including Sundays and recesses of not exceeding five days, and the mileage provided by law; the Speaker of the House of Delegates and President of the Senate shall each receive seven dollars per day for the same period and the mileage provided by law; and the other officers and employees shall receive such compensation for their services as the General Assembly may prescribe. Provision may be made for compensation at said rate of four dollars per day of members of legislative committees which may sit during any recess of said session.

SEC. 21. The compensation and duties of the Clerk of the House of Delegates and of the Clerk of the Senate shall continue as now fixed by law until the first day of January, nineteen hundred and three, after which date their compensation shall be as prescribed by section Sixty-six of this Constitution.

SEC. 22. When the General Assembly convenes on the fifteenth day of July, nineteen hundred and two, its members and officers, before entering upon the discharge of their duties, shall severally take and subscribe the oath or affirmation prescribed by section Thirty-four of the Constitution. And not later than the twentieth day of July, nineteen hundred and two, the Governor and all other executive officers of the State, whose offices are at the seat of government, and all judges of courts of record, shall severally take and subscribe such oath or affirmation; and upon the failure of any such officer, executive or judicial, to take such oath by the day named, his office shall thereby become vacant. Such oaths or affirmations shall be taken and subscribed before any person authorized by existing laws to administer an oath. The Secretary of the Commonwealth shall cause to be printed the necessary blanks for carrying into effect this provision, and the said oaths and affirmations so taken and subscribed, except of the members and officers of the General Assembly, shall be returned to and filed in his office; and those taken by the members and officers of the General Assembly shall be preserved in the records of the respective houses.

SEC. 23. The official copy of the Constitution and Schedule, and of any ordinance adopted by the Convention, shall, as soon as they shall be enrolled, be signed by the President and attested by the Secretary of the Convention, and the President will thereupon cause the same to be delivered to the Secretary of the Commonwealth, who will file and preserve the same securely, among the archives of the State in his custody.

The Secretary of the Commonwealth will cause the Constitution, Schedule, and said ordinances to be transcribed in a book to be provided for the purpose and safely kept in his office.

The Secretary of the Convention will immediately upon the adoption of this Schedule, deliver a certified copy of the Constitution and Schedule, and of said ordinances, to the Governor of the Commonwealth.

SEC. 24. The Governor is authorized and directed to immediately issue his proclamation announcing that this revised and amended Constitution has been ordained by the people of Virginia, assembled in Convention, through their representatives, as the Constitution for the government of the people of the State, and will go into effect as such, subject to the provisions of the Schedule annexed thereto, on the tenth of July, nineteen hundred and two, at noon, and calling upon all the people of Virginia to render their true and loyal support to the same, as the organic law of the Commonwealth.

SEC. 25. This Constitution shall, except as is otherwise provided in the Schedule, go into effect on the tenth day of July, nineteen hundred and two, at noon.

This Schedule shall take effect from its passage.

www.bookjungle.com email: sales@bookjungle.com fax: 630-214-0564 mail: Book Jungle PO Box 2226 Champaign, IL 61825

The Codes Of Hammurabi And Moses
W. W. Davies

QTY

The discovery of the Hammurabi Code is one of the greatest achievements of archaeology, and is of paramount interest, not only to the student of the Bible, but also to all those interested in ancient history...

Religion   **ISBN:** *1-59462-338-4*   **Pages:** 132   *MSRP $12.95*

The Theory of Moral Sentiments
Adam Smith

QTY

This work from 1749. contains original theories of conscience amd moral judgment and it is the foundation for systemof morals.

Philosophy   **ISBN:** *1-59462-777-0*   **Pages:** 536   *MSRP $19.95*

Jessica's First Prayer
Hesba Stretton

QTY

In a screened and secluded corner of one of the many railway-bridges which span the streets of London there could be seen a few years ago, from five o'clock every morning until half past eight, a tidily set-out coffee-stall, consisting of a trestle and board, upon which stood two large tin cans, with a small fire of charcoal burning under each so as to keep the coffee boiling during the early hours of the morning when the work-people were thronging into the city on their way to their daily toil...

Childrens   **ISBN:** *1-59462-373-2*   **Pages:** 84   *MSRP $9.95*

My Life and Work
Henry Ford

QTY

Henry Ford revolutionized the world with his implementation of mass production for the Model T automobile. Gain valuable business insight into his life and work with his own auto-biography... "We have only started on our development of our country we have not as yet, with all our talk of wonderful progress, done more than scratch the surface. The progress has been wonderful enough but..."

Biographies/   **ISBN:** *1-59462-198-5*   **Pages:** 300   *MSRP $21.95* www.bookjungle.com *email: sales@bookjungle.com fax: 630-214-0564 mail: Book Jungle PO Box 2226 Champaign, IL 61825*

The Art of Cross-Examination
Francis Wellman

QTY

I presume it is the experience of every author, after his first book is published upon an important subject, to be almost overwhelmed with a wealth of ideas and illustrations which could readily have been included in his book, and which to his own mind, at least, seem to make a second edition inevitable. Such certainly was the case with me; and when the first edition had reached its sixth impression in five months, I rejoiced to learn that it seemed to my publishers that the book had met with a sufficiently favorable reception to justify a second and considerably enlarged edition. ..

Reference   ISBN: *1-59462-647-2*   Pages:412
MSRP *$19.95*

On the Duty of Civil Disobedience
Henry David Thoreau

QTY

Thoreau wrote his famous essay, On the Duty of Civil Disobedience, as a protest against an unjust but popular war and the immoral but popular institution of slave-owning. He did more than write—he declined to pay his taxes, and was hauled off to gaol in consequence. Who can say how much this refusal of his hastened the end of the war and of slavery ?

Law   ISBN: *1-59462-747-9*   Pages:48
MSRP *$7.45*

Dream Psychology Psychoanalysis for Beginners
Sigmund Freud

QTY

Sigmund Freud, born Sigismund Schlomo Freud (May 6, 1856 - September 23, 1939), was a Jewish-Austrian neurologist and psychiatrist who co-founded the psychoanalytic school of psychology. Freud is best known for his theories of the unconscious mind, especially involving the mechanism of repression; his redefinition of sexual desire as mobile and directed towards a wide variety of objects; and his therapeutic techniques, especially his understanding of transference in the therapeutic relationship and the presumed value of dreams as sources of insight into unconscious desires.

Psychology   ISBN: *1-59462-905-6*   Pages:196
MSRP *$15.45*

The Miracle of Right Thought
Orison Swett Marden

QTY

Believe with all of your heart that you will do what you were made to do. When the mind has once formed the habit of holding cheerful, happy, prosperous pictures, it will not be easy to form the opposite habit. It does not matter how improbable or how far away this realization may see, or how dark the prospects may be, if we visualize them as best we can, as vividly as possible, hold tenaciously to them and vigorously struggle to attain them, they will gradually become actualized, realized in the life. But a desire, a longing without endeavor, a yearning abandoned or held indifferently will vanish without realization.

Self Help   ISBN: *1-59462-644-8*   Pages:360
MSRP *$25.45*

www.bookjungle.com email: sales@bookjungle.com fax: 630-214-0564 mail: Book Jungle PO Box 2226 Champaign, IL 61825

QTY

	Title	ISBN	Price
☐	**The Rosicrucian Cosmo-Conception Mystic Christianity** by *Max Heindel* The Rosicrucian Cosmo-conception is not dogmatic, neither does it appeal to any other authority than the reason of the student. It is not controversial, but is: sent forth in the, hope that it may help to clear... *New Age/Religion Pages 646*	ISBN: 1-59462-188-8	$38.95
☐	**Abandonment To Divine Providence** by *Jean-Pierre de Caussade* "The Rev. Jean Pierre de Caussade was one of the most remarkable spiritual writers of the Society of Jesus in France in the 18th Century. His death took place at Toulouse in 1751. His works have gone through many editions and have been republished... *Inspirational/Religion Pages 400*	ISBN: 1-59462-228-0	$25.95
☐	**Mental Chemistry** by *Charles Haanel* Mental Chemistry allows the change of material conditions by combining and appropriately utilizing the power of the mind. Much like applied chemistry creates something new and unique out of careful combinations of chemicals the mastery of mental chemistry... *New Age/Business Pages 354*	ISBN: 1-59462-192-6	$23.95
☐	**The Letters of Robert Browning and Elizabeth Barret Barrett 1845-1846 vol II** by *Robert Browning and Elizabeth Barrett* *Biographies Pages 596*	ISBN: 1-59462-193-4	$35.95
☐	**Gleanings In Genesis (volume I)** by *Arthur W. Pink* Appropriately has Genesis been termed "the seed plot of the Bible" for in it we have, in germ form, almost all of the great doctrines which are afterwards fully developed in the books of Scripture which follow... *Religion/Inspirational Pages 420*	ISBN: 1-59462-130-6	$27.45
☐	**The Master Key** by *L. W. de Laurence* In no branch of human knowledge has there been a more lively increase of the spirit of research during the past few years than in the study of Psychology, Concentration and Mental Discipline. The requests for authentic lessons in Thought Control, Mental Discipline and... *New Age/Business Pages 422*	ISBN: 1-59462-001-6	$30.95
☐	**The Lesser Key Of Solomon Goetia** by *L. W. de Laurence* This translation of the first book of the "Lernegton" which is now for the first time made accessible to students of Talismanic Magic was done, after careful collation and edition, from numerous Ancient Manuscripts in Hebrew, Latin, and French... *New Age/Occult Pages 92*	ISBN: 1-59462-092-X	$9.95
☐	**Rubaiyat Of Omar Khayyam** by *Edward Fitzgerald* Edward Fitzgerald, whom the world has already learned, in spite of his own efforts to remain within the shadow of anonymity, to look upon as one of the rarest poets of the century, was born at Bredfield, in Suffolk, on the 31st of March, 1809. He was the third son of John Purcell... *Music Pages 172*	ISBN: 1-59462-332-5	$13.95
☐	**Ancient Law** by *Henry Maine* The chief object of the following pages is to indicate some of the earliest ideas of mankind, as they are reflected in Ancient Law, and to point out the relation of those ideas to modern thought. *Religion/History Pages 452*	ISBN: 1-59462-128-4	$29.95
☐	**Far-Away Stories** by *William J. Locke* "Good wine needs no bush, but a collection of mixed vintages does. And this book is just such a collection. Some of the stories I do not want to remain buried for ever in the museum files of dead magazine-numbers an author's not unpardonable vanity..." *Fiction Pages 272*	ISBN: 1-59462-129-2	$19.45
☐	**Life of David Crockett** by *David Crockett* "Colonel David Crockett was one of the most remarkable men of the times in which he lived. Born in humble life, but gifted with a strong will, an indomitable courage, and unremitting perseverance... *Biographies/New Age Pages 424*	ISBN: 1-59462-250-7	$27.45
☐	**Lip-Reading** by *Edward Nitchie* Edward B. Nitchie, founder of the New York School for the Hard of Hearing, now the Nitchie School of Lip-Reading, Inc, wrote "LIP-READING Principles and Practice". The development and perfecting of this meritorious work on lip-reading was an undertaking... *How-to/New Age Pages 400*	ISBN: 1-59462-206-X	$25.95
☐	**A Handbook of Suggestive Therapeutics, Applied Hypnotism, Psychic Science** by *Henry Munro* *Health/New Age/Health/Self-help Pages 376*	ISBN: 1-59462-214-0	$24.95
☐	**A Doll's House: and Two Other Plays** by *Henrik Ibsen* Henrik Ibsen created this classic when in revolutionary 1848 Rome. Introducing some striking concepts in playwriting for the realist genre, this play has been studied the world over. *Fiction/Classics/Plays 308*	ISBN: 1-59462-112-8	$19.95
☐	**The Light of Asia** by *sir Edwin Arnold* In this poetic masterpiece, Edwin Arnold describes the life and teachings of Buddha. The man who was to become known as Buddha to the world was born as Prince Gautama of India but he rejected the worldly riches and abandoned the reigns of power when... *Religion/History/Biographies Pages 170*	ISBN: 1-59462-204-3	$13.95
☐	**The Complete Works of Guy de Maupassant** by *Guy de Maupassant* "For days and days, nights and nights, I had dreamed of that first kiss which was to consecrate our engagement, and I knew not on what spot I should put my lips..." *Fiction/Classics Pages 240*	ISBN: 1-59462-157-8	$16.95
☐	**The Art of Cross-Examination** by *Francis L. Wellman* Written by a renowned trial lawyer, Wellman imparts his experience and uses case studies to explain how to use psychology to extract desired information through questioning. *How-to/Science/Reference Pages 408*	ISBN: 1-59462-309-0	$26.95
☐	**Answered or Unanswered?** by *Louisa Vaughan* Miracles of Faith in China *Religion Pages 112*	ISBN: 1-59462-248-5	$10.95
☐	**The Edinburgh Lectures on Mental Science (1909)** by *Thomas* This book contains the substance of a course of lectures recently given by the writer in the Queen Street Hall, Edinburgh. Its purpose is to indicate the Natural Principles governing the relation between Mental Action and Material Conditions... *New Age/Psychology Pages 148*	ISBN: 1-59462-008-3	$11.95
☐	**Ayesha** by *H. Rider Haggard* Verily and indeed it is the unexpected that happens! Probably if there was one person upon the earth from whom the Editor of this, and of a certain previous history, did not expect to hear again... *Classics Pages 380*	ISBN: 1-59462-301-5	$24.95
☐	**Ayala's Angel** by *Anthony Trollope* The two girls were both pretty, but Lucy who was twenty-one who supposed to be simple and comparatively unattractive, whereas Ayala was credited, as her Bombwhat romantic name might show, with poetic charm and a taste for romance. Ayala when her father died was nineteen... *Fiction Pages 484*	ISBN: 1-59462-352-X	$29.95
☐	**The American Commonwealth** by *James Bryce* An interpretation of American democratic political theory. It examines political mechanics and society from the perspective of Scotsman James Bryce *Politics Pages 572*	ISBN: 1-59462-286-8	$34.45
☐	**Stories of the Pilgrims** by *Margaret P. Pumphrey* This book explores pilgrims religious oppression in England as well as their escape to Holland and eventual crossing to America on the Mayflower, and their early days in New England... *History Pages 268*	ISBN: 1-59462-116-0	$17.95

www.bookjungle.com email: sales@bookjungle.com fax: 630-214-0564 mail: Book Jungle PO Box 2226 Champaign, IL 61825

Title	ISBN	Price	QTY
The Fasting Cure *by Sinclair Upton* — In the Cosmopolitan Magazine for May, 1910, and in the Contemporary Review (London) for April, 1910, I published an article dealing with my experiences in fasting. I have written a great many magazine articles, but never one which attracted so much attention... *New Age/Self Help/Health Pages 164*	1-59462-222-1	$13.95	
Hebrew Astrology *by Sepharial* — In these days of advanced thinking it is a matter of common observation that we have left many of the old landmarks behind and that we are now pressing forward to greater heights and to a wider horizon than that which represented the mind-content of our progenitors... *Astrology Pages 144*	1-59462-308-2	$13.45	
Thought Vibration or The Law of Attraction in the Thought World *by William Walker Atkinson* — *Psychology/Religion Pages 144*	1-59462-127-6	$12.95	
Optimism *by Helen Keller* — Helen Keller was blind, deaf, and mute since 19 months old, yet famously learned how to overcome these handicaps, communicate with the world, and spread her lectures promoting optimism. An inspiring read for everyone... *Biographies/Inspirational Pages 84*	1-59462-108-X	$15.95	
Sara Crewe *by Frances Burnett* — In the first place, Miss Minchin lived in London. Her home was a large, dull, tall one, in a large, dull square, where all the houses were alike, and all the sparrows were alike, and where all the door-knockers made the same heavy sound... *Childrens/Classic Pages 88*	1-59462-360-0	$9.45	
The Autobiography of Benjamin Franklin *by Benjamin Franklin* — The Autobiography of Benjamin Franklin has probably been more extensively read than any other American historical work, and no other book of its kind has had such ups and downs of fortune. Franklin lived for many years in England, where he was agent... *Biographies/History Pages 332*	1-59462-135-7	$24.95	

Name

Email

Telephone

Address

City, State ZIP

☐ Credit Card   ☐ Check / Money Order

Credit Card Number

Expiration Date

Signature

Please Mail to: Book Jungle
PO Box 2226
Champaign, IL 61825
or Fax to: 630-214-0564

ORDERING INFORMATION

web: www.bookjungle.com
email: sales@bookjungle.com
fax: 630-214-0564
mail: Book Jungle PO Box 2226 Champaign, IL 61825
or PayPal to sales@bookjungle.com

Please contact us for bulk discounts

DIRECT-ORDER TERMS

20% Discount if You Order Two or More Books
Free Domestic Shipping!
Accepted: Master Card, Visa, Discover, American Express

www.ingramcontent.com/pod-product-compliance
Lightning Source LLC
Chambersburg PA
CBHW081225170426
43198CB00017B/2715